GIVE'EM THE PICKLE

PICKLE

...and they'll be back!

AN
ABSOLUTELY
CERTAIN WAY
TO BUILD
YOUR
BUSINESS
AND LIVE A
HAPPIER LIFE

ROBERT E. FARRELL
WITH BILL PERKINS

GIVE 'EM THE PICKLE
© 1995 by Bob Farrell

Published by Farrell's Pickle Production Inc.
7165 SW Fir Loop #200
Portland, OR 97223
503-684-2803

Printed in the United States of America.

International Standard Book Number: 0-9648621-0-7

96 97 98 99 00 01 02 03 04 - 10 9 8 7 6 5 4 3 2

Acknowledgments

In a very real sense this book has taken my entire life to write. It flows from a lifetime of experiences. And it flows from a lifetime of relationships.

I want to thank my wonderful wife, Ramona. We've had over 44 years together and I'm looking forward to 40 more. I never could have experienced success in the business world without her loving support.

I also thank my three daughters, Kathy, Colleen and Kristie. They have turned out to be wonderful women, wives and mothers. They made me proud.

I want to thank my first partner, Mr. Ken McCarthy. The success at Farrell's Ice Cream Parlours would never have occurred without him. He made it all happen—down to the last detail. We worked together and made a great team. Thank you, Kenny!

There is a special place in my heart for another partner who came along just when we needed him, Mr. Dale Belford. He brought to the Farrell's organization the administration and financial wisdom needed to make it grow. Dale was in his fifties when he came aboard. But to watch him work, you would have thought he was 35. Dale has gone to be with his Maker, but I still want to acknowledge his critical role.

I must also thank Joe Rutten and Jack Fecker for all they contributed to Farrell's as our first franchise members. There were so many of our early employees and francisees that added to our success: Carla Herring, Rose-Marie Law, Bob Garland, John Ortman, Al Hooning, Paul Lindstedt, Howie Reckstad, and others helped set the standards of running our restaurants. I know I've left some names out that probably should be mentioned, but not intentionally. Thanks to all of you!

I joined up with other good restaurateurs and financiers including: Robert MacLellan, Alan Fleenor and Frank Orrico. Each of them gave 100% of themselves to the business. Because of them we've had other successes such as Newport Bay and Stanford's Restaurants & Bar-two restaurant chains in the Pacific Northwest which are growing to this day.

Most of all I want to thank the thousands of people, young and old, who have worked for our different companies throughout the years. Without them, the 157 restaurants we've opened, would have failed. I'm proud that we've never had a restaurant fail, and they're the reason. Thank you, each and every one for the Farrell's, Engine House Pizza, Newport Bay, Stanford's, Billy Heartbeats, Portland Yogurt, and Portland Deli.

I also want to thank the wonderful customers we've been able to serve. You're wonderful and I thank God for you!

I also want to extend a special thanks to Bill Perkins who pulled this book together. Shortly after Bill and I met, it became obvious we thought alike. Bill has worked in restaurants and is a published author and skilled communicator. He not only took my material and fleshed it out, he added helpful insights and stories. Thanks, Bill.

The sources I used to locate the quotes and sayings didn't list authors so if a quote is yours, or you know the source, let me know so I can include the name in the next printing.

Finally, thanks to Terry and Susan for all the typing, grammatical and spelling corrections and Dave Abraham for helping with the editing.

I hope you enjoy reading this book. I know one thing for sure, when you've finished the last page, you'll possess the insights needed to help you gain more success than you ever thought possible.

Contents

Chapter 9

Chapter One

Value the Customer

If you only read the first few lines of this book, I want you to walk away knowing two things. First, the customer is the boss. Second, the three most important words you'll ever hear from a customer are "I'll be back."

Over the course of my life I've helped open 133 Farrell's Gay Nineties restaurants, co-founded four more successful restaurant chains, appeared on numerous television talk shows, completed the New York Marathon and appeared in a movie. I have to tell you that I credit all of my business success to the grace of God and a deep-rooted belief that the customer is the boss.

No matter what your background, or present experience, you, too, can build a business that magnetically pulls customers back time after time. It's all a matter of taking those two principles and integrating them into every facet of your business so that they characterize the company culture.

The greater the dreams, the higher the obstacles.

I have to warn you, this book isn't about a technique. I'm not giving you a gimmick. I'm sharing with you an infectious value that must capture you and those on your team. Only as you believe, from the depths of your heart, that the customer is the boss, will you make the decisions necessary to bring them back.

My mother built that value into my life when I was a boy. What she gave me I passed on to every manager, hostess, server, cook, and bus-boy I rubbed shoulders with. I hope I have done as well with others as she did with me. I'll tell you more about her later.

I've often wondered if I really didn't get my flare for business from my grandfather, "Old Man" Patrick Farrell. He once owned the largest number of automobile supply houses in New York City. He had outlets scattered from Brooklyn to the Bronx. His business might have survived the economic crash of '29 except that his warehouse in the Bronx burned down. After the fire the "Old Man" learned that his chief financial officer had embezzled the money that was intended for insurance. Without insurance, everything was lost.

Grandfather Pat didn't realize how bad the economic crash was until later. He had loaned money to a lot of friends during the automobile days to help them start a business or keep one afloat. He figured the time had come to call in those loans. Unfortunately, everyone else was going broke faster than he could collect his money. The "Old Man" lost everything but his determination. He started over again and sold oil lubricants until he was over eighty years old.

A ROUGH BEGINNING

That tragedy led to an even greater one. One day, when I was four years old, my mother, sister, and I returned home from a walk and found my farther on the floor—dead. He had taken his own life. To this day I don't know why my dad took his life. My mother doesn't talk about it much. I guess when my grandfather lost his business my dad couldn't handle the pressure of making it on his own. Like hundreds of others in those days, suicide must have seemed like the best solution to his problems.

The following two years of my life were a blur. The next thing I remember is my mother leaving my sister and me at an orphanage. There was no welfare in those days and that was how people got by. The truth is, I received no harm whatsoever from the four years I spent there. The name of the orphanage was Leake Watts, and it still exists up in Yonkers, New York. Today I suspect I gave those poor people a harder time than they gave me. I know I was a handful. I still remember crying when I arrived at the orphanage and crying when I left. Those wonderful folks showed me a lot of love.

When I was almost nine, my mother mar-

ried an English gentleman named Edgar Orpin
and our family was reunited. After being raised
in Brooklyn and Yonkers, we moved "up town"
to Long Island.

THE GREATEST LESSON I EVER LEARNED

Some people might think I had a hard childhood. But I don't remember it that way. I'm one
of those fortunate people who learned at an early
age that even hard times are beneficial. In fact, I
learned the most important business lesson of my
life during my early childhood.

Before moving to Long Island we lived in
Brooklyn. Our apartment was only four blocks
from Ebbets Field. Like the other boys in the
neighborhood, I loved to watch the Dodgers play.
If I couldn't go to a big league game, then I
wanted to play stickball in the street.

One day in April of '37 my mother insisted I
go shopping with her. I begged her to let me go
to a Dodger game, but she grabbed my hand and
marched me out of the apartment. Back in those
days boys wore short pant suits until they were
eight or nine years old. Getting that first pair of
long pants was a step into adulthood. Mom took
me with her because she was going to buy me my
first long-pants-suit. We took the subway to
Manhattan and made the purchase.

♦

Never forget:
THE CUSTOMER
IS THE BOSS!

♦

I thought we might go home after that, but she wanted to buy a pair of pink gloves for the Easter parade. Macy's Department Store was a hub of activity, but the sales clerks at the accessory department weren't too busy. My mother spotted the pair she wanted through the glass counter and waited for some help. A short distance away two sales girls chatted, unaware of my mother's presence. Mom cleared her throat. The girls looked up for a moment and then returned to their conversation.

By that time a fire was burning inside my mother which I'd seen before. To get the clerk's attention she took a large set of keys out of her purse and banged them on the glass counter, almost breaking it.

Here we go again, I thought to myself. I had seen this routine many times before and knew what was coming.

Both clerks looked up when they heard the keys hit the glass.

Mom signaled one of them to come over and said, "And I mean now!" The noise of the keys, the look on my mother's face, and the tone of her voice told that girl she had better hurry.

My mother stood nose to nose with that sales-clerk and asked, "Do you know who I am?"

Confused, the girl said, "No, I'm afraid I don't."

"Well, let me tell you who I am," my mother said. "I'm a customer! Do you understand? And do you know why you're here today?"

The clerk gazed at my mother with a puzzled look on her face. "Well, I work here," she replied.

"That's the wrong answer!" my mother barked back at her. "The right answer is that YOU'RE HERE TO SERVE ME, THE CUSTOMER. Now, I would like to look at those pink gloves," she said, pointing at the gloves in the counter.

As a child I watched my mother do that to retailers from downtown Brooklyn, all through Manhattan and up to the Bronx. My mother taught me the greatest lesson I ever learned in retail sales: THE CUSTOMER IS THE BOSS!

"YOU ARE HERE TO SERVE ME,
THE CUSTOMER, THE BOSS!"

THE KEY TO SUCCESS

That single truth is so powerful it can bring success to someone with limited training and experience. I know because it worked for me. I never even finished high school. In my senior year I was caught impersonating a science teacher, and he had me thrown out of school. I probably wouldn't have graduated anyway. At the time I was kicked out I was flunking almost every subject. I thought school was boring. Instead of graduating with my class, I stood alone and watched my friends receive their diplomas. I have to admit that was a sad day in my life.

Rather than waiting to be drafted I joined the Air Force in 1946. In the testing of my aptitude, the Air Force decided I should become a radar technician. I thought, What a joke! But even though I felt that way, it was a turning point in my life. I became close friends with some ambitious young men. They were different than the boys I had grown up with. Instead of loafing, they enjoyed the rewards of hard work.

After serving in the Air Force I went back to school and earned a high school GED diploma and an Associate of Arts degree in business. On July 28, 1951, I married Ramona Rod in Seattle, and we later moved to Portland, Oregon, where Farrell's Ice Cream Parlours were started.

As I look back over my past I now know what equipped me to be successful. It certainly wasn't an ideal home life or education. The one thing that set me apart was a burning conviction that if I ever went into business for myself—the customer would be my boss!

THE BIRTH OF FARRELL'S ICE CREAM PARLOURS

It's funny how life's unexpected experiences sometimes shape a person's destiny. One Sunday afternoon I was dying for a hot-fudge sundae. My wife, Mona, and I couldn't think of a single place in Seattle where we could get good ice cream on a Sunday afternoon. Finally, I remembered that the Olympic Hotel had served delicious hot-fudge sundaes at a banquet I'd attended.

With a burst of energy I rounded up the kids, piled them into the car, and headed for Seattle. Twenty minutes later we were seated in a plush red booth in the dining room of the Olympic Hotel.

Decked out in formal attire, the waiter approached our family and asked, "What will you have today?"

"We would like five hot-fudge sundaes." I said. "We've already had dinner, and we're starved for ice cream."

The waiter silently stared at me. A moment later he lifted his chin, and disdainfully asked, "Is that *all* you want?"

Immediately, something exploded inside of me. The tone of his voice implied we had committed a social crime by ordering an inexpensive dish in his plush restaurant. I managed to keep my cool, but it wasn't easy.

Later, when we walked out of the hotel, I turned to Mona and said, "Why on earth do waiters treat customers so poorly? Don't they realize customers like me are the key to their success? I've entertained grocery trade meetings here with as many as 200 people. And that guy puts me down because I ordered five hot-fudge sundaes!"

At that point in time I made a decision that changed my life. I told Mona, "There aren't any good ice cream parlours in Seattle—Nice places where families are treated right no matter what they order. I swear, I'm going to start one!"

"IS THAT ALL YOU ARE HAVING?"

◆

Words you want every customer to say: "I'll be back!"

◆

A DIFFERENT TIME AND PLACE

Five years later in Portland, Oregon, I shared my dream with a friend, Ken McCarthy. Because Ken worked for the Carnation Ice Cream Company, he was enthused by the thought of an old fashioned ice cream parlour. In fact, he'd already been talking with some other dairy men about the same idea.

A short time later we opened the first Farrell's Ice Cream Parlour. From day one we decided earning money would never be the primary goal of our business. Instead, our ambition would be serving our customers with excellence! We believed if we did that the money would follow. And it did!

YOU'RE NOT IN BUSINESS TO MAKE MONEY!

We weren't alone in elevating the customer to such a lofty position. In their exceptional book, *In Search of Excellence,*[1] Thomas Peters and Robert Waterman Jr. studied sixty-two of the most successful companies in the United States. Their research included such companies as Hewlett-Packard, IBM, Texas Instruments, Westinghouse, Xerox, General Electric, Hughes Aircraft, McDonald's, Marriott, American Airlines, and Wal-Mart, just to name a few. Without exception, every successful company

1 *In Search of Excellence,* Thomas J. Peters and Robert H. Waterman Jr., Harper & Row, 1982, p. 156

they examined placed a high value on the customer.

Any time making money becomes more important than serving the customer, serious problems occur. Why? Because when the bottom line drives a company, they'll start cutting back on service and quality to make a few extra dollars. When that happens, the customer suffers.

Making money is the result of running the business well, it's the report card. If we take care of the customer, the profit will follow.

A friend, Bob MacClellan, had an experience which illustrates what I mean. While in Los Angeles working on a real estate deal, Bob completed his business and decided to enjoy dinner at a well known restaurant at Marina del Ray. The hostess extended a warm greeting and told Bob there would be a 40-45 minute wait. That didn't seem too long, especially considering the hour. Bob headed for the lounge to have a drink and wait for a table. But before getting to the lounge, he noticed five empty tables. Surprised, he returned to the hostess and said, "Young lady, I see five empty tables over there. Why can't I sit there?"

In a matter-of-fact tone, the hostess said, "We never use those tables on Tuesday."

"Why not?" Bob asked.

"Because we're never busy on Tuesdays," she replied.

That surprised Bob, who wondered why he had to wait if they weren't busy. "Young lady," he said, "you are busy. Why don't you open up those tables?"

"Because there isn't anyone to wait on them," she replied. "We always have fewer waiters come in on Tuesdays, because business is slow."

"Well, if you'd just give each waiter an extra table, you could open up that entire room and take care of the waiting list," Bob said.

Once more, the hostess tried to help Bob understand that those tables weren't used on Tuesdays.

By that time, Bob could see what was happening. The restaurant was cutting back on help to keep their overhead low. And who suffered? The customer!

Any good restaurateur will tell you that's ridiculous. It's far better to have a little extra help and take care of the public than to save a few dollars and make the customer wait. Yet, that's a typical situation where a business values money more than customers.

AN UNEXPECTED ORDER

With a twinkle in his eye, Bob asked the hostess, "Do you mind if my friend and I wait at one of those tables instead of the lounge?"

"Go ahead," she said.

Bob sat down with his friend and took a phone out of his briefcase. He then called information and asked for a phone number. A moment later he dialed Domino's Pizza and ordered an extra large pizza with pepperoni, extra

◆

The man who gets ahead does more than is necessary—and keeps on doing it!

◆

cheese, and pineapple.

In precisely 25 minutes, as advertised, the pizza was delivered. A sharp young man carrying a large thin box entered the restaurant. Bob caught his attention and had the box brought to his table. A moment later the two men were eating a delicious Domino's pizza at the same table the restaurant refused to serve.

Needless to say, the hostess was upset. The poor girl had never seen anything like this. Unsure what to do, she marched to the back of the restaurant in search of the manager. A few minutes later the two of them approached Bob and his associate.

"You can't eat that pizza here," the manager said.

"Why not?" Bob asked. "You weren't using the table, so I thought I would."

After a brief conversation, Bob and his friend ended up on the Marina del Ray dock, where they ate their pizza and watched the sailboats glide by.

While I don't know the identity of that restaurant, I doubt they're still in business. The customer, not the bottom-line, should dictate what we sell, when we sell it and how many people are needed to sell it. A business that honors the customer will never regret it.

A PERSONAL PET PEEVE

Some businesses seem to enjoy doing things that dishonor customers. Several years ago I

◆

Wouldn't it be nice to be as sure of anything as some people are of everything?

◆

needed some cash and stopped at the bank where I have a checking account. I stepped up to the counter and was warmly greeted by an attractive young woman.

"I need to cash a check; do you have a pen?" I asked.

"Yes I do," she replied, and handed me a pen that was attached to the counter with a chain. I suppose I wouldn't have been as irritated if the chain hadn't been so short. I grabbed the pen and discovered I couldn't quite reach my check with it.

"Why do you have pens on chains?" I asked the teller.

"If we don't," she answered, "people will take them."

"Would that be so bad?" I inquired. "The name of the bank is on the pen. If people took one they'd have a nice piece of advertising in their home or office."

"I don't make the rules," the girl replied.

"No, I guess you don't," I said with a smile as I ripped the pen right off the chain.

"Why did you do that?" she asked, backing away as though I might be dangerous.

"Because I want your boss to know that at least one customer feels this bank should be giving away pens, not putting them on chains."

Can you imagine entering a bank with a sign posted in front of every teller that reads: "YOU'RE A THIEF! AND WE KNOW IT." No president or bank manager would ever tolerate such a sign. Yet, putting pens on chains says the same thing.

Ironically, after that experience I read about a bank in California that was walking away with most of the NEW business in the area. Why? According to the article, the bank was growing because they gave pens and roses to every new customer. Even after the opening celebration, they didn't attach pens to chains. Instead, they gave them away. Whoever ran that bank was reaping the benefit of treating the customer like the boss.

YOU GOTTA OWN THE VALUE

You know as well as I do it's easier to say the customer is the boss than to treat them like the boss. It's critical that this simple concept become a value that permeates *every person* in the organization—beginning at the top.

Every day when we get up, we should look in the mirror, and say to ourselves: The customer is my boss! There are days when I feel great and those words energize me. When I feel terrible that sentence keeps me focused. But regardless of how I feel—I constantly remind myself that the customer is my boss.

Let's not kid ourselves. When you're in our business, customers can really beat you up. That's why we have to stop and think, "Why are we really in business?" We are in business to please the next person who walks through our front door. End of conversation! As Nike says, "JUST DO IT."

IT TAKES TEAMWORK

I think of our business as a wheel. Although I'm in the restaurant business, the illustration applies to any business that serves people. The rim consists of the tables, chairs, dishes, pots and pans, equipment, and everything else needed to make the restaurant operate. In other words, the building and equipment. The spokes of the wheel are the different jobs—the waiters, waitresses, bus-boys, bartenders, pantry people,

hostesses, cooks, chefs, dishwashers and everyone else needed to make the restaurant function.
The manager is the hub of the wheel. He's the one who holds all the spokes together and forms the team.

If one spoke of the wheel doesn't pull its load, then the entire wheel will start to wobble. To prevent this from happening every spoke must be tightly secured by the belief that the customer is the boss. The hub must hold the entire wheel together with that same glue. The rim must be kept even by that belief. If it starts to wobble, it will collapse. In fact, any business will ultimately fail if it doesn't concentrate on the customer.

The best way to build a team is to be sure the entire team is focused on the same objective. That is, taking care of the customer. Whether customers are pencil pushers, bean counters, production people, sales persons, truck drivers, it doesn't make a difference. Everyone needs to realize everything they do effects the customer a certain way. If it is negative, we better get it changed. The main goal for all of us is to satisfy the customer better than anybody else.

As the wheel goes down the highway it can carry the business to success if every part is held together by the conviction that the customer is the boss. Building such a wheel begins by personally integrating that value into your life. As you do that, a second value is necessary.

Without the next step, the people on your team will lack the enthusiasm needed to build a successful business. Turn the page and we'll explore the second value and discover how to cultivate it.

Chapter Two

Care for Your Employees

It's critical that you and everyone on your team believe the customer is the boss. That's fundamental. But those who work for you must also believe they're as important to you as the customer. Nothing empowers employees more than a belief that they're valued by their boss— or those they work for. EMPLOYEES MUST KNOW THEY MATTER.

If there's one lesson I've learned in the business world, it's that people work hard when they enjoy what they're doing. It's easy to think that money is the primary motivation for most people. It isn't! People are motivated by a belief that they and their work are important. They're invigorated by people who help them do their job well and then affirm their efforts. I'm convinced people want to have fun at work as much as they want to make money.

The question is: How do we help those on our team enjoy their work? The answer to that question is priceless. If everyone who works in a

◆

A person rarely succeeds at any-thing, unless they have fun doing it.

◆

restaurant is having fun, customers will want to come back. The same is true in every line of business. Enthusiasm has a magnetic appeal.

So, how do we do it? How do we help our employees enjoy their work? I'm convinced we do it by showing them we care.

TAP INTO YOUR PAST

All of us can look back on our lives and identify people who helped us grow by expressing concern for our welfare. I know I can. As a boy I loved to work. I used to set up pins in the bowling alley. I caddied at the golf course. I sold Christmas trees. I worked in various restaurants washing dishes, busing tables, cooking and serving as a waiter. I did anything I could to earn an honest buck.

Sometimes the things I did for fun weren't so honest. My buddies and I used to go down to the local dime store and have contests to see how many yo-yos we could swipe. Some of us would steal so many we would sell a few and use the money we made to have our names etched in the remaining ones by a hired person in the dime store.

I'm not proud of the next story, but it's worth telling. One day three friends and I borrowed a boat belonging to one of the fellow's dads and puttered around Long Island Bay. When I say borrowed, I mean his dad didn't know we had the boat. After spotting a vacant

Nothing is more expensive than ignorance in action.

hunting cabin, we beached the boat, and broke into the house. Inside we found four shotguns and several boxes of ammunition.

We took the guns outside, climbed back into the boat, and circled the cabin shooting out the windows and doors. Actually, we were playing like John Wayne and James Cagney. When we finished having fun, we returned the guns and went home, thinking: What a fun day!

But someone had seen us. They wrote down the identification number of the boat and called the police. The police quickly picked up the boy whose dad owned the boat. Before long, I heard a knock on my front door. Fortunately, my mother wasn't home.

At the police station we got a big break. A friend of the man who owned the cabin, Jack the local barber, knew us kids. He sat down and talked with us. Jack wanted to know why we had shot up the house. He knew we were basically good kids who were acting foolishly. He believed in us. Later on he talked to the owner for us. They agreed to let each of us pay $5 a month until all of the damage had been paid for. It took us three years to pay off that debt—remember, that was 1941 when $5 was a lot of money.

I'm thankful to this day for Jack because he took an interest in us...and I'm sure, kept us from ever going to a reform school. While I haven't had any employees shoot up my home or a restaurant, I've had plenty who needed someone to let them know they cared. That experience prompts me to treat others in the same way I was treated. Never forget, how we treat our employees is exactly how they will treat our customers. Remember, people work because they matter and customers come back for the same reason.

All of us have memories we can tap into to help us understand those who work for us. Empathy is important because it helps us understand how our employees feel. But expressing concern for them has to go further. We have to train them to do their jobs with excellence.

MAKE TRAINING A PRIORITY

Someone who doesn't know how to do their job well isn't going to enjoy their work. Since that's the case, it's imperative that we provide the best training available. We never stop training no matter how much of it we've done.

How is that done? In addition to teaching an employee how to perform a task, such as cooking a steak or waiting on a table, encourage them to take personal steps that will accelerate their growth. When they make a mistake, that's no time for a meeting. Instead, move alongside them and show them what they should do the next time. Practice management by walking around.

Urge them to attend seminars by paying for the cost. We also provide our employees with an extensive library of video and audio tapes on a wide variety of subjects.

HELP THEM FEEL GOOD ABOUT THEMSELVES

If we care about someone we want them to feel good about themselves. We want to infect them with a sense of self-worth. The importance of doing that was driven home to me in a fresh way several years ago when I received a Christmas card from a young man who worked at one of our restaurants. On the inside of the card he scribbled a brief note: "THANKS FOR HELPING ME GROW UP!"

Curious as to what he meant, I paid him a visit. After we had chatted for a few minutes I asked, "What did you mean on the Christmas card when you said I had helped you grow up?"

He smiled and said, "You helped me grow up by teaching me to enjoy my work. You taught me to be ahead of time rather than on time. You had me dress sharp and before long I took better care of my appearance. You instilled in me a desire to make the customer happy instead of just thinking about how much money I could make."

I walked away from that meeting with a deep sense of gratification. That young man didn't feel used. He knew that working for us was more than just a job where he could earn some money. We cared about him, and he knew it. Actually, an employee should be a better person for having worked for us. If not, we've failed.

BE A CHEERLEADER

Nothing I do as the head of a company is more important than leading the team in cheers. That's why after 30 years in the restaurant business I make it a point to regularly meet with every employee. During those times together I ask the question, "Who's the customer?"

Everyone yells back, "The boss!"

I then ask, "What are the three magic words?"

And they shout, "I'll be back!"

But being a cheerleader involves more than leading in cheers. Whenever I eat in one of our restaurants I always try to go back to the kitchen and thank everyone for providing me with such a wonderful meal. I walk around the entire restaurant personally thanking every employee.

I never eat in one of our places with my family as though I had been elected king of the hill. The people who work in our restaurants aren't subservient to me. I know I couldn't succeed without them, but they could without me. And I never want them to forget how much I appreciate them.

DON'T BE AFRAID OF THE "D" WORD

Some businesses treat their employees like pieces of machinery. For those companies training is the equivalent of changing the oil in a car—it has to be done to keep the car running.

◆

The best way to forget your problem is to help someone solve theirs.

◆

But people aren't machines. They think and feel and act on their own. Since that's the case, they need to be taught to live within boundaries. Such discipline frees people to work harder and enjoy their work more.

The other day someone asked one of our waitresses, "Do you like working here?"

Not only did the young woman say she loved working for us, she explained why. Her answer might surprise some people. She said, "I like it here because they're tough. They demand that we do things correctly. They insist we wear a starched shirt or blouse. I have to keep my hair neat and my shoes have to be clean and white. We have to follow certain steps in serving a customer, and we're not allowed to change those steps. We have to memorize every order without writing it down. I don't just serve those customers who sit at one of my tables. I'm available to serve them all.

"In other words," she said, "they're tough, and they make me adhere to all the rules. **THEY HAVE STANDARDS THAT ARE NON-NEGOTIABLE.**"

"You like that?" her friend asked. "Why?"

"Because I make a lot of money," she said. "The restaurants I worked in before lacked discipline and the customers didn't get taken care of so they didn't come back. Here we work as a team and have fun. We love our bosses and they love us—and that's a great thing to know."

HOW DO YOU SPELL DISCIPLINE?

I'm convinced discipline is spelled L-O-V-E.
You know darn well if you don't discipline your
children they'll go haywire. They'll become
unruly and end up in trouble or dying prema-
turely. Most juveniles in jail will say, in so many
words, I wish someone had been around to say
"No you can't go out tonight!"

I recently pulled into a gas station and a big
man with a black beard pumped gas for me. He
looked at me and asked, "Are you Mr. Farrell?"

"Yes I am," I replied.

He told me his name and asked if I remembered him.

I gazed at him for a moment and said, "No, I
don't."

"Why, I didn't think you'd ever forget me,"
he said. "I worked at your Raleigh Hills Farrell's
Ice Cream Parlour."

"I remember a lot of kids from that store, but
I just don't remember you. How long ago did you
work there?" I asked.

"About 18 years ago," he replied.

"I'm afraid I had so many people working for
me I can't remember them all."

Disappointed, he said, "I thought you'd
never forget."

"Gee, I'm sorry." I said. "Why do you think
I wouldn't forget you?"

He then told me his story. He worked on
the training crew at the Fremont, California

Luck is always against the person who depends on it.

store and was on the bus I took down there from
Portland. He said he drove me crazy singing rock
and roll songs.

I told him, "I remember those days, but darn
it, I don't remember you."

"Why wouldn't I forget you?" I asked again.

"Because you fired me!" he blurted out.
"You caught me smoking marijuana in my hotel
room and sent me home on the bus. You even
called my mother and father and they met me
when I got back to Portland. I never forgot that
and didn't think you would either."

"Now I remember!" I said, watching him
more closely. I hoped he had calmed down since
he was a boy. He still had his hand on the gas
pump and I wondered if he wasn't thinking about
dousing me with gasoline.

When he finished pumping my gas he
walked over to my window and said, "I've been
wanting to thank you for what you did for me."

"But I thought you were upset," I said.

"I'm not upset," he replied.

He then told me that when he got home his
parents really let him have it. He pointed to two
boys who were his sons. He said they never
touch marijuana and neither does anyone who
works for him.

"I want to thank you for what you did that
day," he said. "I was ashamed and realized that
smoking marijuana had ruined my summer. I
didn't want to ruin my life so I never touched it
after that."

Sending that boy home was hard for me to
do. Calling his parents wasn't easy. But it was
the loving thing to do. It told him I cared. And
that's a message he never forgot.

GIVE STANDING OVATIONS

While discipline is important, so is recognition. One day I received a phone call from a
woman named Reva. I told her I didn't know
anybody by that name.

She immediately said, "I'm Wilma's daughter."

Wilma was the first cook I ever hired. I
knew she had to be getting up there in years and
feared Reva would tell me her mother had died.
Instead she invited me to her mother's 83rd
birthday party.

"We're planning to have it at the old
Farrell's Ice Cream Parlour next Saturday," she
said.

"Wonderful," I replied. "Let me host the
party and I'll see if I can find others who worked
with Wilma to come with me."

I hung up the phone and pulled out my old
files to see how many people I could invite.

On Saturday a car drove up with Reva
behind the wheel. After it stopped, Wilma got
out, walking with two canes. I could see she had
aged. But one thing hadn't changed—she still
had the happiest smile I have ever seen. Wilma
was a wonderful old-time cook. We hugged,

◆

These three remain: faith, hope and love. But the greatest of these is love.

1 Corinthians 13:13

◆

kissed, sat down and talked. We laughed about the old times for hours.

A few days later I received the following letter:

Mr. "Dear" Bob Farrell,
There was no way to say I could of had a happier birthday. It was such a nice sur-prise. It was great of you and Mona to take time for me on a holiday, since it was the Fourth of July. Reva and I took pic-tures of the sign that said, "Wilma! Farrell's First Cook! Happy Birthday!" I know we will have fun when we use the gift certificate from Newport Bay. The Newport Bays are beautiful restaurants. But not as attractive as the original Farrell's, which was my life.
Thanks so very much,

Truly Yours,
Wilma Byland

Wilma is gone now. But what she said in that letter, I'll never forget. She said, "the origi-nal Farrell's, *which was my life*." You see, the peo-ple who work for us are giving us their lives. Sure, we're paying them. But these are wonder-ful people, and we have to view them that way.

I know it sounds corny, but I loved Wilma. She did a lot for me. There are a lot of wonder-ful people who work for you. I believe we have an obligation to these people to give them the best we can. The best we can afford.

Chapter Three

Hire the Best Managers in the Business

In Alice in Wonderland, when Alice comes to the junction in the road that leads in different directions, she asks the Cheshire Cat for advice.

"Cheshire Puss...would you tell me please, which way I ought to go from here?"

"That depends a good deal on where you want to get to," said the Cat.

"I don't much care where..." said Alice.

"Then it doesn't matter which way you go," said the Cat.

That grinning feline spoke words of truth, didn't he? If we don't know where we want to go, then any road will take us there.

When we opened the first Farrell's restaurant, we knew which way we wanted to go—we wanted to build a restaurant where the customer would return. I've learned over the years that not just any road will get you there. The good news is that once you've set that goal, you can

achieve it. And nothing is more important to
achieving it than hiring the best managers you
can find. That's true regardless of the kind of
business you're in.

WHAT DO YOU LOOK FOR?

I recently read about how the HMS *Titanic*,
which sunk on April 15, 1912, was located on
the floor of the North Atlantic. The find wasn't
the result of luck, just hard work. Robert Ballard
and his colleagues became scholars of the tragedy
by pouring over the eyewitness accounts and
dozens of books about the disaster. A marine
geologist by profession, Ballard spent years ana-
lyzing the ocean bottom in the shipwreck area
500 miles east of Newfoundland. After narrow-
ing down the likely location of the ship, the
painstaking search of the ocean floor began.
Ballard said when a riveted metal cylinder five
times the height of a man appeared on a video
monitor, "We knew we had found the *Titanic*."

All of that hard work wouldn't have meant a
thing if Ballard and his team hadn't known what
they were looking for. In the same way, finding
good managers begins with knowing what they
look like.

BALANCED LIKE A TRIPOD

I've always said when I look for a good manager I try to find someone like a tripod—with
three balanced skills.

• Like a visionary, they must see the customer as the boss and know how to build that value into the business.

• Like an engineer, they must cause things to happen without falling apart.

• Like an accountant, they must make sure the money is available and profits are being made.

If you can find someone with those three traits, you would have a good manager.

PLAYER COACHES

I've also compared good managers to winning coaches. Like a coach, they have to know every player and be sure they're in the right position. Elbert Hubbard said, "There is something that is much more scarce, something finer by far, something rarer than ability. It is the ability to recognize ability." A good manager has a way of helping ordinary people accomplish extraordinary things. They do this by spotting hidden potential and bringing it to the surface.

One way this is done is through careful training. Good managers, like player coaches, don't simply tell everyone what to do, they show them how to do it.

I believe a manager must be the pacesetter of the organization. He sets the attitude of the business. I have found it to be absolutely true that the workers will imitate their managers. If managers care for those on their team, the players will care for each other and serve the customer with greater enthusiasm.

Most of the things worth knowing aren't taught, they're caught!

THE POWER OF LOVE

I believe our managers may be the closest thing to a mother or father many of the young people who work for us have. You see, in the restaurant business we hire an awful lot of young people. We hire more juveniles, uneducated adults and foreigners, than any other business I know of. The manager who treats their employees with love will have a team of people who will do anything for them. And their hard work isn't for money, it's in response to kindness.

I tell our managers it costs them nothing to show kindness to the people who work for them. When a waiter arrives, I urge our managers to greet them with a warm, "Hello," and call them by name. Late at night, when a waitress leaves, genuine concern can be expressed by telling her, "Nice job tonight, Janet. Take it easy going home...and thanks!" Many of the people who work with us have no one else who treats them that way.

My friend, Bill Perkins, worked his way through college as a waiter at a Steak 'N Ale restaurant in Austin, Texas. One night he served a table of 20 people. The party required a lot of attention for almost three hours. Of course, Bill was eager to give them that attention because he expected a big tip.

When the party left, Bill was angered to find less than a dollar in change on the table. Instead of pocketing the money and forgetting about it,

◆

Be kind.
Remember,
everyone you
meet is fighting a
hard battle.

◆

he clenched his fist around the change, walked over to the side door, and threw the money at the customers. "You forgot your change!" he yelled at them as they walked toward their cars.

Needless to say, that didn't make those people too happy. They stomped back into the restaurant and demanded to talk with the manager, Roy Nunis. Roy patiently listened to their complaint and managed to calm them down. Before they left, he gave them a certificate for a free dinner.

Even though Bill had worked for Roy for three years, he thought he'd be fired. Instead, Roy sat down with Bill and asked him, "Do you want to continue to work here as a waiter?"

Bill assured him he did.

"Then you'll have to do two things," Roy said. "You'll have to paint the fence behind the restaurant and you'll have to work as a busboy for two weeks."

Roy treated Bill like a son. Not only did Bill work there for two more years, he learned a lesson that affected the rest of his life. Love has the power to change people. It also creates a setting where employees work harder and serve the customer better.

WHO GETS THE CREDIT?

Former president Ronald Reagan used to have a plaque on his desk which read: There's no limit to what a man can do if he doesn't care who gets the credit. If you substituted the word manager for the word man you'd have a good description of another attitude I look for in a manager. Managers need to be people who aren't worried about who gets the credit. They have to be willing to sacrifice in order to help others succeed.

Back in the early 1900s a young athlete named James Rector of Hot Springs, Arkansas, was a track star at the University of Virginia. When he was chosen to compete in the 1908 Olympic Games in London, he was the favorite to win the 100 meter race.

Rector was one of the first runners in the world to use the crouch stance when starting a race. A week before the games the South African coach approached Rector and said, "We have a great runner, Reggie Walder. I shouldn't ask you this, since he'll be competing against you, but would you teach him how to start from the crouch stance?"

James Rector had to make a tough decision. He hesitated a moment, and then said he'd be glad to help Walder.

Almost a hundred years later, the record book shows that Walder learned very well. He beat Rector and went on to fame. But behind Walder was the man who sacrificed a gold medal to help him win.

I believe that every good manager has that same attitude toward the rest of their team.

They recognize it's their job to help others succeed—no matter who gets the credit. That's why
the policy in our restaurant is: Every customer is
everyone's—every table is yours.

MANAGEMENT BY WALKING AROUND

Of course a manager can't build a winning
team if he's locked up in an office somewhere.
Managers need to be out there where the people
are. At United Airlines, Ed Carlson labeled it
"Visible Management" and "MBWA—
Management By Walking Around."

I tell our managers to grab the coffee pot and
walk around the dining room. After they've
done that, they should put the coffee pot down
and wander around the back to see what's going
on in the kitchen. How is the person washing
the dishes doing? How are the waiters and waitresses feeling? They should look for opportuni-
ties to lend a helping hand. If they can help provide better service, then they should do so.

No business can be run from an office. The
manager has to be out there with the rest of the
team. He needs to be with the customer. We
call it carpet time.

One of the greatest examples I ever read
about involved Eddie Carlson. He was the president of Western Hotels when that company
merged with United Airlines, and he became
president of the airline. Mind you, this man who
started out as a bellhop at the Olympic Hotel in

The most valuable gift is a good example!

Washington, became the president of one of the largest airlines in the world. Someone might ask, "What did he know about airlines?"

When he became the president of United he knew very little. But he also knew he'd never find out if he stayed in an ivory tower. Over the next eight months, he took his top executives and visited every hanger United used and every airport they served. They not only met the people in each location, they asked questions. Specifically, they wanted to know how they could run the airline better. They asked how the employees were doing. They tried to find out how they could better serve them.

When they returned home they had filled several books with information on how to run an airline better. But something else happened. The rank and file in the business had met their president, and they liked him. He seemed to genuinely care about them. He had visited them in New York, Miami and Chicago. HE MANAGED BY WALKING AROUND.

THINK ON THEIR FEET

Good managers will also have the ability to think on their feet. Sometimes that will mean breaking the rules, or at least bending them. If they see a policy isn't helping serve the customer, they won't be afraid to change it. They'll have enough confidence to make those decisions because they'll realize some policies don't apply to their situation.

I remember the story of the man whose wife was preparing a roast for dinner one night. As he watched her he was surprised to see her cut off both ends of the roast before putting it in the oven.

Curious, he asked, "Why did you cut off the ends of the roast?"

She smiled and told him she had learned how to cook a roast from her mother who, "Always cut off both ends before placing it in the oven."

When he pressed her, he discovered she didn't really know why the ends of the roast were cut off.

The next time he saw his wife's mother he asked her the same question. To his surprise, she had learned how to cook a roast from her mother who, "Always cut off both ends before placing it in the oven."

Determined to get to the bottom of this, he called his wife's grandmother and asked why she had taught this cooking technique to her daughter and granddaughter. The elderly woman laughed and said, "I had to cut off the ends of the roast so it would fit into the oven."

Sometimes policies are like that. At the time they were formulated they served a good purpose. But a good manager will have the sense to know when that purpose isn't being served any more.

FLEXIBILITY

Managers have to be able to make snap decisions. That means they can't be afraid of making mistakes. An inability to make quick decisions can hurt the customer.

I like the story about the young man who managed the produce department of a large grocery store. One afternoon a woman tapped him on the shoulder and said, "Young man, I would like very much to have one half of a grapefruit."

The manager smiled and graciously said, "I'm sorry, but we don't sell grapefruits by the half. But they are on special today, and you can buy three for $1."

The lady looked at him indignantly and said, "Young man, I've heard your television and radio ads for this supermarket. And those ads said this store belongs to me—the customer. Now I want half of a grapefruit. I live alone in an apartment. I only need that much and I want to buy it right now."

The manager realized he needed to bend the rules at this point in order to satisfy this customer. He picked up a grapefruit and told her he'd be back in a minute. In the back room he took a knife and sliced the grapefruit in two.

As he was returning to the woman, the store manager stopped him and asked, "Harold, what are you doing with half a grapefruit? Are you going to use it on a display?"

The produce manager said, "No, this old biddy approached me as I was spraying the fruit and asked for half a grapefruit. When I told her we didn't sell grapefruit that way, she let me know that this supermarket belonged to her, just like our ads said. Anyway, I have this grapefruit for that old hag."

Just as those words left his mouth, the produce manager looked in the mirror and saw the lady standing directly behind him.

Without a moment's hesitation, he turned around and said, "And this nice lady would like the other half."

After taking the grapefruit, the woman walked away with a big smile on her face. The store manager turned to Harold and said, "I liked the way you handled that. That woman went away pleased even though you said what you did."

After a moment's thought, the manager went on, "Harold, we're building stores across North America and Canada. You've been doing such a good job that I'm going to suggest you become the manager of the newest store in Saskatchewan, Canada. What do you think of that?"

With a disgusted look on his face, Harold said, "Who wants to live in Saskatchewan? There's nothing up there but ladies of ill-repute and hockey players!"

"Young man," the manager said, "I'll have you know my wife lives in Saskatchewan."

The produce manager immediately said, "You're kidding. What hockey team did she play on?"

I can't help but laugh every time I hear that story. But the story is more than entertaining, it also illustrates the value of being able to think on your feet.

I suppose if I was going to summarize what you should look for in a manager I would do so with a short list I found a number of years ago. It describes the most important words in life.

IMPORTANT WORDS TO LIVE BY

THE SIX MOST IMPORTANT WORDS:
    "I admit I made a mistake."

THE FIVE MOST IMPORTANT WORDS:
    "You did a great job."

THE FOUR MOST IMPORTANT WORDS:
    "What is your opinion?"

THE THREE MOST IMPORTANT WORDS:
    "I love you."

THE TWO MOST IMPORTANT WORDS:
    "Thank You."

THE LEAST IMPORTANT WORD:
    "I."

Chapter Four

Little Things Make Big Impressions

Joe Girard understood the value of little things. That's why he sold more cars and trucks, each year, for eleven years running, than any other salesman in the country. His devotion to detail has brought him international recognition.

Joe committed himself to service. But not just service—service in the little things. After a customer bought a car, Joe's son would write them a Thank You note before they were out the door. A year after a sale, Joe would personally talk with the service manager on behalf of his customer.

Joe refused to let his customers forget him. Every month throughout the year he sent them a letter. Each arrived in a plain envelope that was a different size and color. When they opened it, they immediately saw the words, "I LIKE YOU." Inside it said, "Happy New Year from Joe Girard." In February he sent a card wishing the customer a "Happy George Washington Birthday." In March it said, "Happy St. Patrick's Day." With service like that, no wonder Joe Girard sold so many cars!

No matter what line of business you're in, it's the little things that satisfy customers. And they're the reason customers say, "I'll be back."

THE SPOKES ON A WHEEL

As I mentioned in chapter one, I like to think of our business as a wheel. The rim consists of the things that make the restaurant operate—the equipment and building. The spokes are the different jobs that have to be done. The manager is the hub of the wheel. He holds the spokes together.

In this chapter I'd like to examine each spoke, or job, and see how it helps the wheel run smoothly. While I'm in the restaurant business, I think you'll see that the various jobs in a restaurant represent roles which exist in every business that serves people, including yours.

FIRST IMPRESSIONS

In most good restaurants you're greeted by a host or hostess shortly after you walk in the door. We want eye contact to be made with a customer within seven seconds after they enter the restaurant. A prompt and warm greeting tells the customer we're glad they came. When you're exceptionally busy, smile, raise an eyebrow or wink in

◆

You never get a second chance to make a first impression!

◆

order to let them know you care. It assures them
they'll have an enjoyable evening. Customers
entering any business want to be noticed, and
hopefully recognized, as soon as they enter. No
one likes to be the invisible man.

The value of first impressions can't be over-
stated. This is true in business and in life. I
remember when I was in the air force a couple of
buddies and I drove into Seattle one night. Just
south of town we spotted a place called The
Spanish Castle, which was a dance pavilion that
featured a band called Gorden Green and His
Orchestra. We went inside and found the place
filled with attractive young women.

I spotted a good-looking blonde and asked
her to dance. She was gracious, and the two of
us stepped out onto the dance floor. I asked her,
"What's your name?"

"Ramona," she said.

Thinking of a famous song about an Indian
maiden, I wondered if this blonde haired blue-
eyed girl was an Indian. "Romana is an Indian
name," I said. "Is it your real name?"

She told me it was and I asked about her last
name.

"My last name is Rod."

"Rod?" I said.

"Yes, Rod." she replied.

"Your real name is Ramona Rod. I've never
met anyone with a name like that. What do you
do, Ramona?" I asked.

"I'm a riveter at Boeing" she replied.

"You mean, you're Ramona Rod the riveter? I don't believe it."

By then we were both laughing, and she said, "My name is Ramona Rod, but I'm not a riveter. I'm a private secretary for the gas company."

I have to tell you, Ramona's sense of humor, not to mention her good looks, made a favorable first impression. In fact, she made such a good impression that after our date I knew, "I'd be back." Three years later we were married and we're still together. "Thanks for the dance" was printed on our 44th anniversary cake.

THE HOST OR HOSTESS

In any business, the host or hostess is the first person a customer sees. Their job is to make a good first impression. The host or hostess isn't always a receptionist who greets clients as they come in the door or call on the phone. They could be a truck driver delivering your product. Maybe they're a dock hand loading trucks, or a carpenter framing a building.

Each of these serve as a host or hostess when they're the first person making contact with a customer. We all know that a rude truck driver who runs other cars off the road, beeps his horn or waves an angry fist, doesn't make a favorable impression. And when the trailer he's pulling has the name of your company in block letters on

◆

Our five senses are incomplete without a sixth... a sense of humor.

◆

its side, he's certainly not attracting customers.

We've all had bad experiences with telephone receptionists. Seeking information about a product, we call a business and the person who answers the phone is rude and uninformed. After a few minutes we angrily hang up the phone vowing to never call that store again.

On the other hand, a warm and well informed hostess makes us want to buy the product. They make us feel special. They have the power to make us a good customer or no customer at all.

One of the main reasons a potential customer may come to my restaurant or buy your product is because of the way they're handled on the phone. I tell our people to always smile across the telephone lines. We used to train our hostesses by letting them listen to themselves on the phone by recording them when they least expected it.

THINK OF THE CUSTOMER

At our restaurants we challenge our hosts and hostesses to always remember that the customer is the boss. Their job is to think of the customer first. They need to see life through the customer's eyes.

In his book, *The Psychology of Winning*, Dennis Waitley tells the story about a lady who took her five-year-old son Christmas shopping at a large department store. She knew he would enjoy all the decorations, window dressings, festive music and Santa Claus.

◆

View life through your customer's eyes!

◆

Soon after they arrived the boy began to cry softly and cling to his mother's coat.

"Good grief, what are you fussing about?" she scolded. "Santa doesn't visit cry babies!"

"Oh well, maybe it's because your shoe's untied," she said and knelt down in the aisle beside him to tie his shoe. As she knelt, the woman happened to look up.

For the first time, she viewed her world through the eyes of a five-year-old! She didn't see any bangles, presents, or brightly decorated table displays—just a maze of aisles too high to see over...giant legs, fannies and feet pushing and shoving, bumping and thumping! Rather than looking like fun, it looked terrifying!

She took her child home and vowed to never impose her version of fun on him again.[2]

A good host or hostess will view the world through the eyes of the customer. That's why we tell them to avoid putting a couple next to a noisy party. A man and woman who go out for a romantic evening don't want to be disturbed by a noisy group of people.

If someone is eating alone, we don't want them to be greeted with the words, "How many are in your party?"

The person might say, "I'm by myself."

If the host or hostess replies, "You're alone?" they make the customer feel like everyone is

2 *The Psychology of Winning*, Dennis Waitley, Berkley Books, New York, 1979, p. 23.

staring at them thinking, that poor man or woman, they can't get anyone to eat with them.

A single person should be seated as fast as possible and given a menu or newspaper—something to read, if they want it. I know of one restaurateur who buys people who are alone an after dinner drink. Why? To let them know they're appreciated, even if they're not a big party.

Every customer who walks through that door is our boss, and they need to be given special attention. They need to be treated like the boss.

EVERYTHING IN BETWEEN

Once a customer is seated, the little things take on added significance. Remember, our goal is to satisfy every customer. If we accomplish

"YOU'RE ALONE?"

that goal, we'll make more money than we know what to do with. I've never seen it fail.

THE SECOND SPOKE—THE BUSPERSON

Every company has someone who is out in the front lines taking care of the details that make everything work. In a restaurant, that person is the busboy or busperson. The waiters, waitresses, servers and bartenders are able to do their jobs because these people take care of the little things.

In a factory, this person gets the right tools for a supervisor. In a hospital they make sure the rooms are clean. In a business they're the comptroller who keeps track of the little things.

When I hire buspersons I look for people who like to act on their own. Young people who run track, play tennis, wrestle or play golf, work well in this role because they are used to competing alone.

I believe that in the restaurant business there should never be dirty tables that can be seen upon entering the dining area. Tables should be cleaned before the customer can get out the door. This tells the arriving customers, "We expected you and we're glad you're here."

AVOID THE D.Ts

In the old days we used to have managers who called out, "D.Ts." This meant "Dirty

Tables." A manager would walk the floor, and call out the D.T.s letting his busperson know which tables needed clearing.

One Saturday night I had two ambitious buspersons working who were track stars. They were having fun trying to clean a table before I pointed it out to them.

One time they yelled out, "Table 21 cleaned, Mr. Farrell." No sooner had I seated four people at the table they had just cleaned then the four who had been sitting there came out of the restroom looking for their table. They hadn't finished their meal yet!

Of course, I got them another table and treated them to a meal. But I'd rather do that than have dirty tables.

I believe the owner of any good retail operation will have the same philosophy. If you go into a drug, grocery, or department store, you don't want to see empty boxes on the floor and bare shelves. Every business has their busperson. It's their job to make sure the shelves are well stocked and the store looks attractive when the customer first walks in. They need to realize they're not just cleaning off a table or stocking a shelf, they're getting it ready for the next customer.

THE THIRD SPOKE—
THE KITCHEN CREW

Whether you're manufacturing automobiles, computers, televisions or packaging corn flakes,

Things will probably turn out all right, but sometimes it takes strong nerves just to watch.

the kitchen is where the product is produced and taken care of. It's here that time, quality and costs must be controlled. In a restaurant the product is put together, cooked, and sold within minutes. In most factories the customer isn't involved with the product until much later.

A restaurant has a head chef who is in charge of procuring products. They make sure everything that enters the back door is opened, inspected, weighed and stored.

Once these goods are in storage, they go to the prep people. Their job is to prepare the food according to an exact formula, or recipe. This is done in a clean area as quickly as possible on a routine basis. Rations have to match sales so that there is little left over at the end of the day and the new product is fresh. Everyone in the kitchen must learn all recipes and preparatory methods. Once everything is prepared, the chefs and cooks can quickly prepare the food for a customer. Every ticket in a high-quality restaurant must be put together and served within six to ten minutes. It takes a well oiled system with strong leadership to make this happen.

Regardless of your business, everything that happens behind the scenes must be well organized so that the product presented to the customer is both timely and appealing.

CONSISTENCY

The most important word in a well-run kitchen or any other business is CONSISTENCY. Consistency is a key to customer satisfaction. The customer must believe they can depend on you to give them the same quality every time they return. Once you've established yourself as consistent, they'll keep coming back.

Nobody illustrates this better than McDonald's. Their hamburgers, milkshakes and fries taste the same throughout the world. They have systems that dictate how the fries and hamburgers are cooked. That system is used in every McDonald's from California to Maine and from London to Hong Kong. When you walk into a McDonald's, you know what you're going to get in all 15,000+ locations.

CLEAN DISHES

Our commitment to the little things causes us to even give personal pep talks to our dishwashers. While many chefs and managers started out as dishwashers, it's usually the least skilled and lowest paid job in a restaurant. But their role is crucial because every dish and every piece of silverware will be placed in front of our boss—the customer. If the dishwasher doesn't do a good job then the customer won't say those three magic words, "I'll be back!"

I like to tell our dishwashers about a sharp

young lady who was gifted by God with a beautiful smile that lit up the room. This girl was crazy about a boy in her high school class, and she constantly flirted with him. Finally, he got the hint and asked her out.

The girl was thrilled and spared no expense to make this date a special occasion. She had her hair done and bought a new dress. Before he picked her up she gazed in the mirror and thought, I look great!

At 7 P.M. the doorbell rang, and there he was. He complimented her dress and escorted her out to his car. As they drove to the restaurant they were both a bit nervous. But the tension was eased as she smiled that beautiful smile and laughed at his dumb jokes.

At the restaurant they were seated and ordered their dinner. As dinner was served they laughed and talked, and she thought to herself, He likes me. I can tell he really likes me.

But about half way through dinner, he stopped looking at her. The poor girl wondered, What did I say wrong? Things were going so well, and now he's hardly talking.

The two left the restaurant and drove to the theater without saying much. Later, on their way home he was still silent. At the door, he only gave her a handshake.

Disappointed, the girl ran upstairs into the bathroom and began to cry. As she looked in the mirror she discovered the problem. Across three of her teeth was a large hunk of green spinach.

The boy was too shy to say anything and too embarrassed to look at her. Every time she smiled, he could only see the spinach. He certainly wasn't going to kiss a girl goodnight who had a wad of spinach across her teeth.

I like to tell that story to our dishwashers because when the customer enters our restaurant, it's like going out on a first date. If they enter our beautiful lobby and are warmly greeted by a host or hostess, they're going to feel welcomed. If they're seated at a lovely table and waited on with care they're going to like our restaurant. If the food looks good they'll be pleased. But if they pick up their silverware and for the first time notice a piece of dry lettuce on a fork, or a knife with soap stains, or lipstick on a glass, or a cracked cup, everything else will be wasted. All they'll notice are those soiled articles. Nothing will look right after that.

Everything that's placed in front of the customer has to be perfect! Whether you're selling cars, televisions, beds, clothes or furniture— every thing the customer sees must be just right, or they won't come back. If there's any spinach caught in the teeth of your business, you'd better take care of it now!

FINAL IMPRESSIONS

If first impressions are important, so are final impressions. I used to love working as the

◆

The people who tell you not to worry about the little things, have never tried sleep-ing in a room with a mosquito.

◆

cashier at the original Farrell's Ice Cream Parlour because I enjoyed asking customers, "How was everything?"

THE FOURTH SPOKE—THE CASHIER

Every business has a person who makes the final contact with a customer. I love to hear satisfied customers say, "Everything was great. We'll be back!"

But I also want to hear the truth. I want to find out what things we could improve on to better serve our boss—the customer. I've always trained our people to ask how everything was, and then listen to find out how the customer really feels. Someone may say everything was fine, but the tone of their voice or their body language may give a different message.

If I sense any dissatisfaction, I'll probe for a more complete answer. They may then say, "The coffee was cold!"

Since I know we serve hot coffee, I might discover a burner on the coffee machine is broken. Remember, it's the little things that count. And nobody can point them out to us better than the customer.

I remember once when a couple with a young son was leaving I asked, "How was everything?"

I knew by the father's voice that he wasn't telling the truth when he said, "Everything was fine. How much do I owe you?"

◆

The best way to do better tomorrow is to begin doing better today.

◆

Curious, I said, "Sir, I know something's wrong. I would like to correct it."

He told me it couldn't be fixed. It was too late.

I let him know who I was, and that I would do anything possible to make things right with him.

He was so upset his lips quivered as he shouted at me, "YOU CAN'T STRAIGHTEN IT OUT! IT'S TOO LATE."

I pleaded with the man. "Sir, please tell me the problem."

He then informed me that they had brought their little boy to Farrell's Ice Cream Parlour to celebrate his birthday and to get his free sundae. But most of all, his son wanted everyone to sing for him. The man said he hadn't told the waiter, but he had told the hostess.

Of course, I knew what had happened. The hostess forgot to tell the waiter, and that little boy sat there without a sundae and listened as other children were sung to. The parents were so upset that they didn't even say anything. They were just going to get up and leave.

"Sir, I'm very sorry."

"You ought to be," he said between gritted teeth.

"Well, I'm going to make it up to you right now," I said as I lifted his little boy up on the counter. I grabbed a sundae and handed it to the boy.

Change is a process, not an event.

"What's your name?" I asked.

"Alex!" he said.

"How old are you, Alex?"

"I'm six years old," he said with a big smile.

I turned to everyone in the restaurant and said, "Please turn this way, stop eating and put your utensils down. We're all going to sing "Happy Birthday to Alex, who is six years old today." That family never forgot the fuss we made over Alex.

Everybody stood up, cheered and sang for Alex. They gave him a birthday song he'll never forget.

As Alex's father left, he turned to me and said those three magic words, "We'll be back." And they did come back. It's been over 25 years, and they're still coming back to our restaurants. They never forgot the fuss we made over Alex.

"HAPPY BIRTHDAY!"

Why did we do it? Because little Alex is our boss. Taking care of the little things with people like Alex is the key to building loyal customers.

To make a point on the famous 3 words we want to hear "I'll be back," I'll have you know Alex and his family have continued to come in our restaurant for over 25 years. They never forgot we took care of them the day we blew it on his 6th birthday.

Never forget: You're in business to take care of the customer. When you do that you'll make more money than you ever dreamed of.

Chapter Five

Win Their Loyalty with Your Service

The Green Bay Packers won the first two world championships of professional football by outscoring their opponents in Super Bowls I and II. The Packers were coached by the great fundamentalist Vince Lombardi. When Lombardi's team played poorly, he would begin practice the following week with a basic comment that has become almost as well known as Lombardi's name. "Gentlemen, we performed below the standards we have set for ourselves as a championship football team. This week we're going to return to the fundamentals." Lifting a football he had been holding in his hands to a position above his head, Lombardi would intone in that deep, raspy voice he kept hoarse from shouting at his team from the sidelines, "Gentlemen, this is a football."

No sooner would those words leave Lombardi's mouth than team prankster Max

McGee would call from the back of the room, "Not so fast, Coach, not so fast."

I can just imagine McGee sitting with a pad and pencil in hand writing out the phrase, "This is a football."

REMEMBER THE FUNDAMENTALS

Vince Lombardi knew the value of fundamental truth. Whether it's applied to football or business, fundamental truth always brings the same result—success.

I'm such a devoted Lombardi fan that we used to have Vince Lombardi Manager's Meetings. We'd kick off the meeting by showing a film of the coach's motivational speech. When the film was over I'd stand on a chair with a sundae in my hand and say, "This is a sundae!"

I always used those meetings to recognize the efforts of team players. One of my fondest memories was the day I gave my partner, Dale Belford, a football autographed by the Green Bay Packers. As I have told you earlier, Dale was our senior executive. That day he really appreciated being recognized and honored by all his young peers. HE KNEW HE MATTERED.

Even today a lot of the old Farrell's employees still say, "Don't be on time, be ahead of time." That's one of the great sayings we learned from Coach Lombardi.

Those meetings were important because they provided me with a platform to communicate the fundamentals needed to succeed in business. As you master them, I think you'll also be successful.

THE FIFTH SPOKE ON THE WHEEL— YOUR SALES FORCE

In the last chapter I pointed out four spokes that make up the wheel of every business. In this chapter I'd like to talk about the fifth spoke—the sales force. In the restaurant industry we refer to these people as waiters and waitresses or service people. In your business it's probably the sales person. Ultimately, this is the person who will be responsible for what the customer thinks about you and your company. How they treat the customer will determine whether they make a purchase, how they feel about what they've bought and whether they come back and refer their friends.

I believe an effective sales person can win a customer's loyalty with their service. How is this done? Instead of getting into specific techniques, I want to talk about three fundamental principles that have to be mastered when a customer is dissatisfied. Once these are learned, the techniques will flow from them. Without these three principles, the best sales techniques in the world won't work.

The first principle is this: The customer is always right. I realize that saying has been used so many times it's become trite. Yet, even though that's the case, it's still true. Unless the customer is acting illegally or disrespectfully, they can do no wrong.

THE CUSTOMER IS ALWAYS RIGHT

Several years ago two professional women came into one of our restaurants and ordered white fish. When the fish was served one of the women took a bite and frowned.

A moment later she signaled the waitress who approached her table with a smile. "Young lady, I ordered halibut!" the woman said. "This is cod, and I'm not going to pay for halibut and eat cod."

The waitress realized she had served the woman halibut. The way we prepare the two they can be distinguished because halibut has a dull surface while cod is shiny.

I was standing a few feet away and had watched the waitress take the order, serve the women and field the complaint. I knew the waitress was one of our best, and I was curious to see how she would handle the situation.

"I'm very sorry," the waitress said, "please let me correct this." She then took the plate and I followed as she carried it back to the kitchen.

The waitress told the cook, "John, the customer said this isn't halibut."

John, like any other cook, didn't like being told he had prepared the wrong dish. With a defensive tone he said, "What are you talking about? Of course it's halibut."

"John, I know it's halibut. You know it's halibut. Mr. Farrell knows it's halibut. But our customer doesn't think it's halibut. So John, it's not halibut. Please prepare her a new dish."

Without hesitation, John made a new dish as our chefs are instructed to do in that situation. Our procedure also calls for the manager to return the second dish to the dissatisfied customer.

When the meal was prepared, the manager picked it up, and with the waitress following, placed it before the customer. "I hope this is what you want. I'm very sorry for the mistake."

I smiled as the young woman took a bite of the fish and said, "Mmmmm. Now that's halibut. Thank you very much!"

I'm sure that waitress felt like saying, "So was the first one, Lady." Of course, she didn't. Why? Because she knew the customer is always right.

THE POWER OF FAITH

Earlier in the book I mentioned that a concern for the customer isn't a gimmick. It has to be a value that flows from our innermost being. You might wonder how such an attitude can be cultivated if it's not present. In answering that question, I feel I should share with you a very personal story.

◆

If you wish to be agreeable, you must pretend to be taught many things you already know.

◆

I didn't always feel or express genuine concern for others. In fact, I grew up in a home where there was a lot of yelling, screaming and arguing.

I always had the idea that getting the job done was the most important thing—even if a few people got trampled along the way. I really had no feelings for others and would even lie to make a sale. As a child I watched my mother and father lie quickly and openly if it would help them.

When I was 23 years old I married a wonderful young girl from Seattle, Washington. Ramona grew up in a healthy family where everyone related to each other in a loving way. While we were dating I was able to control my impatience and insensitivity. It wasn't too hard to be polite around the dinner table or on a date. But shortly after we were married my wife saw the real Bob Farrell. I was a loud, pushy kid from New York City. We used to argue about the way I drove, blowing my horn all the time or being discourteous. I remember my children asking what I was mad about. I'd yell at them, "I'm not mad!"

Our marriage was in real trouble, and I knew I was the reason. I wasn't a deeply religious person at the time, but I knew I needed some help. When I read in the newspaper that Billy Graham was going to speak in Seattle on how a couple could have a happy marriage, I decided to go.

The evening I listened to Graham he used the Bible as a marriage manual. He showed how a husband could love his wife and treat her with kindness. He explained how through His death on the cross Jesus died for all the hurtful stuff I had done. I learned that through faith in Christ I could experience forgiveness and receive God's power to change.

That night I entered into a relationship with God, but I didn't tell anyone. Amazingly, God began to change my attitude toward people. I began to treat my wife and children with love. My attitude toward my boss and fellow-workers changed. So did my attitude toward my customers. I wanted to help them—not just make money off of them.

Since then, I've found all kinds of direction from the Bible that has helped me with my business. I don't mean to imply that everyone has to believe as I do in order to run a successful business. Nor do I mean to suggest I don't still have a lot of shortcomings—I do. But I think a relationship with Jesus Christ is critical, because He can enable us to overcome our selfishness and help us love our families, employees and customers. When that happens, the way we treat our customers is an expression of what's truly inside of us. I've also found that my faith in God gives me the security I need to accept criticism.

DON'T EXCUSE IT—FIX IT!

I frequently tell our sales people to never make an excuse for something that's wrong. Customers don't want excuses, they want results. The second principle is simply: Don't excuse it, fix it. If something isn't right it's our job to correct it. While that truth is simple enough, some people have a hard time learning it. In the next story a waiter made a mistake and did something worse than giving an excuse—he refused to admit he had done anything wrong.

Several years ago my friend, Bill Perkins, and his wife, Cindy, were enjoying dinner with some friends in one of the finest restaurants in Portland. The moment they entered the restaurant they were warmly greeted by the hostess. Their table was elegantly set with a candle and fresh flowers. As they talked with their friends live piano music provided a romantic background.

A moment after they were seated, their waiter handed them a menu, told them about the evening's specials and then departed so they could decide what they wanted to order.

HOW DO YOU LIKE YOUR STEAK?

A few minutes later the waiter returned and Bill ordered a steak extrarare. Not wanting to take any chances, Bill said, "Please have your chef cook it 90 seconds on one side, flip it over and cook it 90 seconds on the other side."

The waiter smiled and nodded his head, "It will be precisely as you ordered it," he said.

But it wasn't. When Bill cut into the steak it was cooked medium rare. Way too done for him! He said he knew it was cooked too much when he poked it with his fork, and it didn't quiver.

Bill finally caught the waiter's attention and called him over to the table. "I hate to trouble you," Bill said, "but I ordered this steak extrarare and it's medium rare."

The waiter appeared agitated as he picked up the plate and walked away. A minute later, the headwaiter returned to the table with the steak still on the plate. He showed the steak to Bill and said, "Sir, are you telling me you think this steak isn't extrarare?"

Needless to say, Bill was terribly embarrassed. "It's not cooked like I ordered it," he said. "I asked that it be cooked 90 seconds on a side."

The next thing the waiter did is unbelievable. He took the steak over to the couple eating dinner with Bill and his wife and showed it to them. "Doesn't this steak look extrarare to you?" By that time, the people sitting at the surrounding tables were silently watching this unbelievable ordeal.

Finally, the headwaiter returned with another steak and watched as Bill cut into it. Right away Bill noticed it was a bit too rare, but he fig-

ured he'd rather have it that way than over-
cooked.

"How is the steak?" the waiter asked.

"It's fine," Bill said.

"Well, I'll have you know I made sure it was
only cooked 50 seconds on a side, not 90," said
the waiter and walked away in a huff.

NEVER EMBARRASS A CUSTOMER

The next day Bill called the restaurant and
asked to talk with the manager. You can imagine
his surprise when he discovered the headwaiter
was also the manager.

"Do you always embarrass your customers
like that?" Bill asked.

"But you are the one who embarrassed me!"
the manager said. "Imagine how I felt when you
accused my chef of not cooking your steak prop-
erly."

"Am I hearing you right?" Bill asked. "Are
you telling me you were more concerned with
protecting yourself from embarrassment than satisfying me—a customer?"

At about that time the manager realized
what he had been saying and began to backpedal.
But it was too late. The damage had been done.

That restaurant manager failed to apply a
fundamental principle: The customer is always
right.

People who admit they're wrong get a lot farther than people who prove they're right.

It's one thing to make a sale and another thing to give quality service after the sale. In the restaurant business the service after the sale begins the moment an order is taken. We have to continue to take care of the customer to make sure they're satisfied with what they purchase. In other businesses the lag time is greater, but the need to take care of the customer after the sale is just as great. Regardless of your business, the customer is the boss and can't be wrong.

THE MOMENT OF TRUTH

Every time a customer comes into contact with a company it's a moment of truth. The customer will walk away from that contact feeling better or worse about the company. And, it's how well the employees manage those numerous moments of truth every day that ultimately determines how successful the business will be.

THINK ABOUT THIS

A typical business hears from only 4 percent of its dissatisfied customers. The other 96 percent just quietly go away and 91 percent never return. A survey aimed at finding out why customers don't come back to a business discovered some interesting facts:
- 3 percent move away,
- 5 percent develop other friendships,
- 9 percent leave because they find a better price,

- 14 percent are dissatisfied with the product,
- 68 percent quit because of an attitude of indifference toward the customer by the owner, manager or an employee.

But that's not the end of the story. A typical dissatisfied customer will tell eight to ten people about his problem. One in five will tell twenty. It takes twelve positive service incidents to make up for one negative incident.

Seven out of ten complaining customers will do business with you again if you resolve the complaint in their favor. If you resolve it on the spot, 95 percent will do business with you again. On average, a satisfied customer will tell five people about the problem and how it was satisfactorily resolved. One thing is clear: The best marketing takes place inside our place of business.

Working with the above facts we calculated a dissatisfied customer who doesn't return and who influences others will cost us $24,000 a year in gross sales. Since the best advertising is a satisfied customer, it's surprising that most businesses spend six times more to attract new customers than they do to keep old ones. Yet, the key to keeping old customers is as simple as the fundamental principles: The customer is always right and don't excuse it, fix it.

◆

Don't satisfy your customers— delight them!

◆

NEVER ARGUE WITH THE CUSTOMER

The third principle flows from the first two. Since the customer is always right, and it's our job to fix problems not excuse them, it makes sense that a salesperson should never argue with a customer. Even if the argument is won, the customer is lost.

A friend of mine called me up one day and said, "You'd better call _____ company and suggest they allow you to give them your Pickle Speech." He then told me why he felt that way.

One day his thirteen-year-old daughter went to a local card store to buy a St. Patrick's Day troll doll for a friend's birthday party.

A few days later she found out another little girl had bought the same doll to give to their friend at the party. Heartbroken, she explained the situation to her dad and begged him to return the doll to the store so she could get another one.

Because he frequently shopped there for cards my friend was confident he could take care of the problem. The next afternoon the two of them went back to the store to exchange the doll. My friend explained to the sales clerk what had happened and asked if he could return the doll.

"We do not take back seasonal merchandise!" the woman replied. "This doll has on a St. Patrick's Day hat, and that makes it a seasonal item. I'm sorry, but I can't accept it back."

My friend tried to explain their situation once more. He even pointed out that St. Patrick's Day was still four days away.

"We do not take back seasonal items," the woman insisted.

"But we live a few blocks away," my friend said. "I've purchased many cards and gifts in this store over the years."

"I'm sorry, we do not return seasonal items," the sales clerk repeated.

Realizing he wasn't getting anywhere with that approach, he tried a different one. "Would you be willing to give me a credit for the doll so I can buy something else in the future."

"I'm sorry, we do not return seasonal items," she said. "And I'm not going to repeat myself again." With that comment, the sales woman turned and started talking to another clerk, totally ignoring my friend and his daughter.

Needless to say, my friend left that store seething with anger and determined he would never return. He told me he had already told his story to over 50 people in their neighborhood. Amazingly, that local store is part of a national chain that spends millions a year on advertising to attract new customers.

While that sales clerk won an argument, she lost a customer along with everyone he would tell about what she had done.

It's far better to take the approach demonstrated by a waiter who served a friend and me in

**A man must be big
enough to admit
his mistakes,
smart enough to
profit from them,
and strong enough
to correct them.**

a restaurant several years ago.

When my friend gave his order, he said, "I've noticed the dinner I asked for has onions and I don't want any onions on my plate. May I order it that way? They give me heartburn just looking at them."

The waiter assured him he could. A short time later the waiter served the two hot entrees. The moment the plate was placed in front of my friend he spotted something he hated—sliced onions. He couldn't stand the sight, smell or taste of onions.

With a stern look and a harsh voice he said, "I told you I don't want onions."

That waiter could have said, "You didn't tell me to hold the onions."

He could have made an excuse such as, "I told the cook you didn't want any onions. I even wrote it down so he wouldn't miss it."

Both of those responses would have been wrong.

That waiter did the right thing. He said, "I'm sorry, I should have noticed that." He left and came back with a clean dish and a fresh order. "Here it is sir, just the way you wanted it!"

The server assumed full responsibility for the mistake and then corrected it. As he walked away my friend said, "Now there's a good waiter!" That waiter understood three fundamental principles:

The customer is always right.

Don't excuse it, fix it.
Never argue with the customer.
If you'll build those three simple principles
into your sales force, customers will come back
and bring their friends.

Chapter Six

Give 'Em the Pickle. . .

The title for my book, and this chapter, grew out of an experience I had many years ago. In our first Farrell's Ice Cream Parlour we always invited our customers to let us know how we were doing. When we did something wrong they would write and let us know so we could fix it.

From the beginning we always answered every complaint letter with a personal response, not a form letter. A manager, vice-president or supervisor would respond to every complaint. If a problem was great enough a manager might make a personal phone call or send a gift to the customer. We would do whatever it took to let the customer know we cared.

Occasionally a letter would be addressed to me. One letter from a customer in Seattle became my favorite. Here's what it said:

Dear Mr. Farrell,

I've been coming to your restaurants for over three years. I always order a #2 hamburger and a chocolate shake. I always ask for an extra pickle and I always get one. Mind you, this has been going on once or twice a week for three years.

I came into your restaurant the other day and I ordered my usual #2 hamburger and chocolate shake. I asked the young waitress for the extra pickle. I believe she was new because I hadn't seen her before.

She said, "Sir, I will sell you a side of pickles for $1.25."

I told her, "No, I just want one extra slice of pickle. I always ask for it, and they always give it to me. Go ask your manager."

She went away and came back after speaking with the manager. The waitress looked me in the eye and said, "I'll sell you a pickle for a nickel."

Mr. Farrell, I told her what to do with her pickle, hamburger, and the milkshake. I'm not coming back to your restaurant if that's the way you're going to run it."

The Customer

He signed his name and fortunately for me, included his address. I wrote him a letter and enclosed a card for a free hot-fudge sundae. I assured him we didn't run our business that way, apologized, and asked him to please come back.

I signed the letter and didn't expect to hear from him again.

A year later my wife was flying to Norway and I accompanied her to the airport wearing my Farrell's jacket. As I checked her baggage the young man behind the counter asked me, "Do you work for Farrell's?"

I told him I did.

He smiled and said, "I go there all the time. They're so good. In fact," he continued, "I wrote Mr. Farrell a letter once."

"No kidding?" I said. "Well, that's me."

He looked at my wife's ticket and said, "By golly, you are Mr. Farrell." He then reached out and shook my hand.

"What was your letter about?" I asked.

"Oh no, you wouldn't remember it," he said.

"Tell me about it so I can try."

"It was about a pickle," he said.

I looked at him in utter surprise. "The pickle! I never forgot the pickle story. I've told thousands of people about that pickle."

Curious, I asked him what he did for the airline.

"I'm in charge of customer service at the front counter," he said. "It's my job to make sure everyone flying overseas on our airline has all they need to assure them of a good time."

"No wonder you were angry about the pickle," I said. "You're obsessed with service, and when you didn't get it you got upset."

"Yes, I'm afraid I did," he said.

I thanked him for writing and assured him

his letter has had a far bigger impact than he ever imagined.

KNOW YOUR PICKLES

If there's any one message I want to communicate it's the importance of giving away pickles. The secret of running a good business is a willingness to "Give 'em the pickle." Of course, that means you have to know what a pickle is in your business.

I'll never forget an experience I had after speaking to a group of independent garbage men. A big burly man worked his way through the crowd, walked up to me and grabbed my hand. "I loved your story," he said. "I give pickles away all summer."

STARTING LAWNMOWERS

As he spoke I imagined garbage truck drivers giving away jars of pickles. I wondered if he understood what I was talking about.

"What's your pickle?" I asked.

"My boys and I start lawnmowers," he said.

"What do you mean?"

"We have a system," he explained. "Whenever we see a man or woman cranking away trying to start a lawnmower, we stop our truck and help them out. Over the years we've learned to start every kind of lawnmower. We've made a lot of good friends. And we've added some new accounts and kept some old ones. Our pickle is starting lawnmowers."

I shook that man's hand and said, "That's great. You've definitely got the right idea."

TIRES

I recently talked with my friend, Jack McMillan, co-chairman of Nordstrom, a company cited more than any other as the standard for customer service.

"Are the pickle stories I hear about Nordstroms' true?" I asked.

"What do you mean?" he said.

I then explained that someone told me about a man who brought back a set of tires to Nordstroms'. His wife said she had bought them there, and he couldn't use them.

"Did you really take them back?" I asked. "That's hard to believe since you don't even sell tires."

"Yes, we did," he said. "The Nordstrom brothers are very particular about taking care of the customer."

Mr. Nordstrom once told a group of 1500 employees, "Spend my money. Take care of the customer."

With an attitude like that it's no wonder the customers at Nordstroms' feel so well cared for.

♦

Whether you think you can, or can't— YOU'RE RIGHT

♦

WEDDING CAKES

I love the story about Rich's Department Store in Atlanta, Georgia. One day the store sold a five-tier wedding cake to a young woman. When the cake was baked and decorated it was both beautiful and expensive. When the groom failed to show up at the wedding, the bride thought she would have to eat the cake. Instead, Rich's insisted she return the cake—no charge.

I asked someone at Rich's why they did that. After all, a wedding cake can't be resold. They told me, "No it can't be. But that young woman has enough trouble. She doesn't need to pay for a wedding cake she can't use. And besides, some day she'll get married. I'm sure we'll be making that wedding cake."

VALIDATE THE PARKING TICKET!

Several years ago the *Wall Street Journal* reported on an incident which occurred in Spokane, Washington. A man dressed in dirty coveralls entered a bank and asked a teller to validate his 35 cent parking ticket.

She looked at the man's unshaven face and tattered clothes and asked, "Did you do business in the bank today?"

"No, I didn't," he replied. "I had to run into the drug store next door, and they don't validate parking. I didn't bring any cash with me and hoped you'd validate my parking ticket since I have an account here."

"I'm sorry, sir," the woman replied, "but if you didn't do business in the bank today, I can't validate your parking ticket."

"Well, let's do some business then." The man said.

"Fine, what would you like me to do?" the teller asked.

"I want you to close out my account!"

Startled by his request the teller told him that wouldn't be necessary.

"No, I want my ticket validated," he insisted. "You said I had to do business in the bank to get it validated, and this is the business I want to do."

"Very well," the teller said.

She took the man's name and went to a computer to find out how much money he had in the bank. When the number appeared on the screen her face turned ashen white. She called the manager over and explained what had happened. He then approached the customer and assured him the bank would gladly validate his 35 cent parking ticket without him closing out his account.

"Close the account!" the man insisted.

A short time later he walked out of the bank with over $1,260,000—and a validated parking ticket.

He immediately walked across the street and opened an account in another bank.

◆

Give people more than they expect and do it cheerfully!

◆

That foolish bank teller! She had a chance to give a customer a 35 cent pickle and didn't. You can never tell who a customer is by how they dress. Since that's the case—give them all a pickle.

PEOPLE LOVE TO HEAR THEIR NAME

I've saved one of my favorite pickle stories for the last.

When I was fourteen years old I got a job pumping gas at a local gas station in Oceanside, Long Island. In those days people would pull up to a pump, and the gasoline attendant would ask how much gas they wanted. Nine out of ten customers would say, "Give me a dollars worth."

Of course, when gas only cost 20 cents a gallon, a dollar would buy five gallons of gas. But my boss wanted the customer to fill up his tank, not just buy five gallons.

To accomplish this, he devised an amazing plan that made every customer feel special. He told every attendant to call their customers by their name. When I first heard his instructions, I thought he was joking. After all, hundreds of cars bought gas from him every day.

Here's where the man's genius came in. He had attendants ask the customers their name. We would then take the gas cap into the office and write the name on a piece of adhesive tape and stick it to the underside of the gas cap.

The next time the customer returned, we'd

immediately take off the gas cap, read their name, and greet them personally.

"Mr. Johnson," I'd say, "how about a fill up today?" Almost without exception they'd smile and say, "Sure, son, fill 'er up!"

Those people were amazed and gratified that they were so well thought of at the gas station that every attendant knew their name.

I learned at an early age that people love to hear their name. Once we called them by name, we could sell them fan belts, lights and tires. If we knew their name, we were their friends, and friends can be trusted.

GIVE 'EM THE PICKLE

Whatever your line of business, there are pickles you can be giving your customers. Maybe it's starting a lawnmower, giving away a cake, returning merchandise they bought somewhere else, validating a parking ticket or remembering a name. Whatever that pickle is—be sure and find it. And remember, if you'll Give 'em the Pickle, the customer will know they're the boss and you'll hear them say those three magic words, "I'll be back!"

Chapter Seven

Farrell's Ice Cream Parlour— The Early Days

On a brisk September day in 1963 we opened the first Farrell's Ice Cream Parlour in Portland, Oregon. We originally planned to open on a Wednesday. But when we noticed that Friday of that week was the 13th, we decided to open then.

I laughed and told Ken, "If we don't make it, we can say we were jinxed."

When we opened the doors at 11 A.M. we were shocked to find a line of 85-100 people waiting to get in. What a ride that day started!

LAYING THE FOUNDATION

My first job after getting married was as a sales clerk with H.J. Heinz Company. I thought it would lead to sales. One thing was certain, I didn't belong in an office. I hadn't worked there

◆

Not even a turtle makes progress until he sticks out his neck.

◆

long before my boss came to the same conclusion. He urged me to find a job in sales. Unfortunately, the H.J. Heinz office in Seattle didn't have any sales jobs.

I hit the road looking for a job in an area of Seattle called "food row." I knocked on the doors of Pilsbury, Stokely's and General Foods. Finally, I talked with "Libby Joe" Mr. Joe Fasano at the Libby, McNeil, Libby Company. He hired me even though I didn't have a job. With my enthusiasm he thought he would take a chance. I was hired to go through the Seattle area and get some new baby food accounts. As anybody knows, Gerber owned the baby food business and Heinz was second. In my first seven months I picked up 23 new baby food accounts.

How did I do it? The answer is simple. I gave my customers service they weren't getting from Heinz or Gerber. I came back each week to fill their baby food sections. I even cleaned the entire section including my competitions.

I learned early, if I could give my customers more than they expected, I would get and keep their business. Before long I was the district manager of Seattle and later became the branch manager of Oregon. I built displays, hired demonstrators, dressed up like a clown and hung decorations.

That experience was great preparation for the restaurant business. While I was getting that experience, my future partner, Ken McCarthy, was working as a sales representative for the Carnation Company. He trained people to operate ice cream fountains—perfect preparation for an ice cream parlor!

I had wanted to open an ice cream parlor for some time and when I told Ken my idea, he shared my zeal. I had worked in restaurants and knew a lot about food portions, but hardly anything about ice cream. But Ken knew everything about ice cream.

Once we decided to go into business together we weren't sure the ice cream parlor would make enough money for both of us. So, Ken kept his job and I quite mine to open the first restaurant. That's why my name appeared on the parlor. If Carnation had found out Kenny was a partner, they wouldn't have liked it!

THE LOCATION

Once we made the decision to bring back the old fashioned ice cream parlors to Portland, we had a lot of work to do.

We knew that finding a good location was critical. In college I learned that the best location for a shoe store is next to other shoe stores. The same goes for restaurants.

While we couldn't find a location beside the best restaurant in town, we hit the jackpot anyway. Ken heard about a location underneath a supermarket, with parking beside it. Our job was to sell the owner on the idea that we could run a restaurant well enough for him to invest as our landlord.

On a hot summer day in Portland, Ken and I sat down with Harold Schhnitzer. Harold is a successful owner of shopping centers, apartments, and office buildings. As our potential landlord listened, Ken and I described the kind of restaurant we wanted to open. Little did we know that Harold had a yearning for ice cream sodas. He realized that a lot of people shared his appetite but there weren't any places to get ice cream sodas.

Harold was hooked on the idea. He agreed to finish the inside of the restaurant with the decor we needed, including the lighting, floors and walls. To this day, we're grateful for his help. He saved us between $15,000 and 20,000 (that would be $250,000 today).

Needless to say, Harold did well on his investment. And he deserved it. After all, he gambled on us. And we worked hard to make his gamble pay off. We figured if his return was good, ours would be too. And it was!

Ours was fantastic. We opened our doors with having each invested only $2500 in cash, and sold out 8 years later for that times one thousand in Marriot stock, each.

THE CAST

Remember, we were going to open a turn-of-the-century ice cream parlor. We wanted it to have the feel of 1905. To accomplish that we devised quite a show. The stage was the ice cream parlor and the cast was the employees.

Selecting good employees was critical. Our research indicated we should hire older mature chefs and cooks. We may have overdone it, but it worked. All our wonderful ladies in the back were over 55 years old. Each of them was good natured with a wonderful sense of humor. We knew that their patience would enable them to train the high school and college kids who assisted them. If we were going to cast a 1905 ice cream parlor person, they would have to be young, attractive, ambitious, and well groomed. We found these kids in abundance. Many of them came from Portland State University which was close by.

TRAINING

Once we had assembled our cast, we had to train them. Ken took the back of the restaurant and I took the front. We spent a week training them. Once we felt they understood what they were doing, we had them practice on their friends. We even had a pre-opening dinner where we invited our friends to help get the feel for our opening day. It seemed things were going well.

There were some foul-ups. The kitchen had a hard time getting the food out fast enough. Later, as we opened other restaurants, we realized that happens every time. That's especially true if

◆

If all the world's a stage, a lot of us need more rehearsals.

◆

it's a new concept with a new menu. Even skilled people find it takes time to become acquainted with a new kitchen.

OPENING DAY

I have to admit, I worried for six weeks before our grand opening. I hardly slept. I'd lay in bed, tossing and turning. I sweat so much I had to change pajamas at least twice a night. I didn't fear failure. I feared we'd be too busy. I wasn't sure if we could take care of them. And I was right. They did come. In fact, they couldn't wait to get in. And we weren't ready. In fact, our opening day was a disaster. We did everything wrong. We ran out of ice cream and bananas. I'll bet we bought every banana within a three mile area. We bought all the hamburger the store above us could grind. We cleaned out every hamburger bun, head of lettuce and tomato we could get from area stores. As the weeks went by, the store above us put in a hamburger patty machine just to take care of us.

You might think such an opening day response sounds good. But we knew there were a lot of people who were disappointed in the service and delivery of our food. Fortunately, they had the patience to give us a second chance.

◆

A hard fall is a top bounce if you're made of the right material.

◆

"I'LL BE BACK"

Our first day while I was working at the register, a lady walked right past and looked at me, smiled and left. I wondered, *Why didn't she stop to pay me?*

I went outside and asked, "How was everything? Was the food okay?"

She told me she hadn't eaten because the waitress never came to her table. As I was apologizing she interrupted, "Don't worry, I'll be back."

"Why?" I asked.

Smiling she said, "Because everyone was trying so hard. It's your first day and you have a lot to learn. And because you're out here on the sidewalk being nice to me. With that kind of attitude, I know you'll be a success."

I was sorry we had disappointed her. Our service was horrible. We couldn't get the food out fast enough. The ice cream was too hard. Our first lunch shift was frustrating. When it was over, we all breathed a sigh of relief. If the evening was anything like lunch, we had better be ready.

That first night was big. They started coming in at 5 P.M. and we still had a line out the door at midnight. It never stopped. It was one of the most fantastic days of my life. I hadn't slept for 48 hours, but I was flying high. Even though we had disappointed some, we made a lot of people happy. The customers loved us.

MAKING IT BETTER

We had a number of things we had to fix. One thing was the large post that was in the middle of the dining room. It stood right in front of the counter where the food came out. The post was so large, about a 2 1/2 foot square, that the waitresses hid behind it on opening day. By hiding behind the post they could prevent the frustrated customers from staring at them.

I told the waitresses, "Don't hide. Tell them how sorry you are for the delay. Tell them their order will be out soon. Let them know the problems occurred because we'd just opened."

Unfortunately, the problems didn't go away quickly. During the first month, it sometimes took us 30 minutes to fill an order that should have taken a few moments. We'd occasionally lose a ticket. Those early days were tough!

The young girls would panic. I could see it in their eyes. Some of them would cry. As the business grew, that post became a place for the girls to lean back and sigh.

I encouraged them to go into the freezer, shut the door, and scream as loud as they could. That little suggestion actually helped. They would come out of the freezer with a smile on their faces.

As I've reflected back on that experience, I've wondered if every company shouldn't have a freezer so the employees could go in and scream their head off. It might actually increase production!

Chapter Eight

Farrell's Ice Cream Parlour— Making it Better

It's not widely known that we were the first restaurant to serve hamburgers on onion roll buns. These buns were made for us at a bakery in Portland. It took a while for the bakery to perfect the product. Occasionally the buns would be so tough they couldn't be chewed. We had to keep working on the recipe until we had it correct. And we finally did just that. It was quite funny sometimes watching customers try to bite into one of those tough onion roll buns. They couldn't believe what was happening because the bun smelled and tasted fresh, but were very hard to bite through.

Our candy department was a success from the first day, even though it was meant to be there for atmosphere only. I had ordered about 250 candy sticks from the Pennsylvania Dutch Candy Company. I lined up a ten foot area with different kinds of old fashioned candy not expecting to sell much of it. Once again, our wonderful customers taught us a lesson. By the end of the fourth day, we didn't have three candy sticks left. They had cleaned us out. We phoned the candy company and started ordering multiple cases every few months. They couldn't believe we were selling so much candy. In fact, they were so impressed they sent a representative to our restaurant to find out what we were doing.

Of course, it wasn't a secret. We just put the candy by the cash register. One customer told me, "I have to hand it to you guys. We walk in and our mouths water when we see the candy. Then we sit down and eat dinner. When we're finished, the kids won't let us alone until we buy them some candy."

Eventually, candy sales made up 12 percent of our dollar volume. As the chain grew we ended up selling millions of dollars worth of candy every year.

We tried to make a visit to one of our restaurants as fun as possible. We rang bells, beat the drum and blew the horn. Some people were surprised by all the excitement. One woman took her first step into the store while the bells were ringing, sirens blaring and boys running around with a zoo on their shoulders. She looked around shocked and actually fainted. Fortunately, there was a line of people in front of her and they prevented her from falling to the floor. She never expected such noise in what she thought was a quaint little ice cream parlor.

If you would rule the world quietly, you must keep it amused.

We had a lot of babies cry with fear when we beat the drum and blared the siren. They would get used to our fun and clamor to return.

OUR EARLY EMPLOYEES

In the 60s and 70s we had a lot of talk about how teenagers were going to the dogs. Yet, we had hundreds of them working for us all over the country. They were willing to wear their hair short, starched shirts, clean pants and shined black shoes.

DEVOTED WORKERS

One young man sometimes worked until two or three in the morning. While driving him home one rainy night we saw a figure lying face down at the curb. Both of us thought someone had been hit by a car. We stopped, jumped out of the vehicle and ran over to him. When we turned him over, the boy said, "That's my dad. He's always drunk."

We piled him into the car, took him home and put him to bed.

That young man worked for us for four years, went to college and is now doing well. He accomplished all of that even though he grew up in such a difficult home situation. It's nice to see people turn out well regardless of their situation.

CREATIVE

Sophia was our pantry lady. She never would admit her age, but I think she was in her sixties when we hired her. She had worked for some of the finest hotels and restaurants in Portland. She made the best salad dressings in the area. Eventually we had to put her recipes into writing so we could duplicate them elsewhere.

"But if I do that," she said, "you won't need me any more."

I assured her that we weren't that kind of people but that we needed the recipes for a new restaurant that was opening in Seattle. After all, consistency is important in restaurants.

Sophia agreed and wrote out all of her recipes. One day when she was off work we needed more blue cheese dressing. We had someone make up a batch using Sophia's recipe. But it didn't taste as good.

A few days later while Sophia was making some blue cheese dressing I watched her. When she thought I had turned away she added an extra pound of blue cheese crumbs. That was the difference! She wasn't trying to deceive us. She made the dressing by taste and had written out the recipe from memory. But when she actually mixed the dressing, she didn't think it tasted right until she had added the extra blue cheese. We made the change in writing and were able to duplicate Sophia's dressing.

The same thing happened with Wilma's clam chowder. She gave me a recipe that was popular in Portland. Her recipe called for 3.5% butterfat milk. But when we used the recipe, the chowder didn't taste as good as Wilma's. One day when she didn't know I was looking I saw her add a pitcher full of 32% heavy whipping cream.

She was afraid I was mad at her. I laughed and told her I wasn't mad. But if the whipping cream made the clam chowder good, we wanted it in the recipe.

RESTAURANT ROMANCE

An attractive young couple ate at our Portland restaurant every Friday night. They would hold hands and gaze into each others eyes. They looked like they were sitting on a Hollywood set.

One day the man came in with a different girl. As they sat down, she left for the restroom. When she was gone, I asked the young man what had happened to the other lady. He explained they had an argument and had broken up.

A few hours later his old girlfriend came in with some other girls. I approached her and asked about her boyfriend. She said things had taken a bad turn, and she didn't know where he was.

For several weeks the two came separately

with other friends. Each night I told the fella that the different girls he was bringing in weren't his type. I urged him to get back together with the other girl.

One Saturday night the two came in together. They were holding hands and looking starry eyed. Eventually they were married. Several years later they came back with a baby.

The mother approached me and said so loudly that others in the restaurant could hear, "I wanted to show you what you did, Mr. Farrell."

My face turned beet red. After they left I had to explain to everyone that I had helped get the couple back together. I wasn't the child's father.

THE POWER OF A POSITIVE OUTLOOK

Diana was a bright, young, and attractive waitress. But too often she would be overwhelmed by her circumstances. I repeatedly told her to smile. She would say, "I am smiling."

"No, you're not." I said. "You look like a sourpuss."

"That's because the people who come in here drive me crazy," she replied.

"If you feel that way, you're in the wrong business," I said.

"That's not true!" she replied. "It's just the ones that come into this restaurant."

"The problem is with you," I told her. "You let people get you down. If you're not feeling good when you come in here, try going up to a customer and saying to yourself, '*I like you. I really do.*' If you'll do that you'll be surprised by what happens."

She gazed at me for a moment and then said, "Mr. Farrell, I think you've flipped!"

But she agreed to try it anyway. Later that afternoon she asked, "Mr. Farrell, did you give me every nice customer who came in the restaurant today?"

"No, I didn't," I said. "The difference was in your attitude." She tripled her tips because she had a positive attitude.

GIVING IT YOUR BEST

One of our servers was a great big fellow we called Yogi Bear. He was a happy-go-lucky guy. Sometimes he would let people upset him. In the service business we can't let that happen. They may have their problems when they come in the door, but we need to help them have a pleasant experience.

Almost every Sunday, Yogi Bear would tell me, "I have the same family again with the two brats."

I told Yogi to just take care of them. And he did. That family returned every Sunday with their kids out of control. Once, one of the kids actually threw up all over the table. I told Yogi to clean up the mess with a smile.

Yogi did what he was told. The family

◆

Cooperation:
Doing with a smile
what you have to
do anyway.

◆

apologized as they left. But what I never told
Yogi was that the family always asked to sit in his
section. Yogi told me how he felt about those
kids, but he never let them know. Why?
Because he knew they were his boss.

HAPPY BIRTHDAY!

At the original Farrell's Ice Cream Parlours
we would sing "Happy Birthday" to every child
who told us it was their birthday. On many
Saturdays, I would sing "Happy Birthday" over a
hundred times. I have to admit, there were times
I didn't feel like singing. I learned how to sing to
those kids with a smile on my face, even when I
didn't feel like it.

One day I had sung "Happy Birthday" 124
times. I actually counted. It was getting late and
I was tired after working a double shift. In came
a family with a little boy. He ran up to me and
said, "It's my birthday!"

I felt like saying, "So what?"

But I couldn't do that. That little boy didn't
know I had sung "Happy Birthday" 124 times
already that day. And he didn't have to know.
His parents brought him to Farrell's because it
was the boy's birthday. It didn't matter if I had
sung 300 times or 3,000 times that day. I had to
sing to that boy as though it was the first and
only time that day.

That's true whether you're selling cars, television sets, insurance, real estate or anything else.

The great thing about Farrell's was the pleasure both children and parents experienced.

Nothing is more rewarding than truly meeting another person's needs. It's more gratifying to see others open the gift you've given, than to open the one you've received. In a sense, that's what service is—giving gifts to others.

Chapter Nine

Pickle Stories and More

Over the years I've collected pickle stories, proverbs and anecdotes that have given me both laughter and insight. This final chapter is a treasure chest containing some of my favorite.

A SENSE OF URGENCY

The founder of a highly successful company was asked what it took to succeed. He said, "It takes the same thing it took to get it started—a sense of urgency."

The people who make things move in this world share this same sense of urgency. No matter how intelligent or able you may be, if you don't have this sense of urgency, now is the time to start developing it. The world is full of very competent people who honestly intend to do things *tomorrow*, or as soon as they can get around to it. Their accomplishments, however, seldom match those of the less talented who are blessed with a sense of urgency.

EVERYBODY, SOMEBODY, ANYBODY AND NOBODY

There is a story about four people, called
Everybody, Somebody, Anybody and Nobody.
There was an important job to be done and
Everybody was asked to do it. Everybody was
sure that Somebody would do it. Anybody could
have done it, but Nobody did it. Somebody got
angry about that because it was Everybody's job.
Everybody thought Anybody could do it but
Nobody realized that Everybody wouldn't do it.
It ended up that Everybody blamed Somebody
when actually Nobody asked Anybody to do it.
Please don't let this happen here because we
expect everyone to help!

I AM YOUR CUSTOMER

You often accuse me of carrying a chip on
my shoulder. I suspect this is because you don't
understand me. After all, isn't it normal to
expect satisfaction for your money?

Ignore my wants and I will cease to exist.
Satisfy those wants and I will become increasingly
loyal. Add to this satisfaction a little personal
attention and a friendly smile and I will become
a walking advertisement for your restaurant.

When I criticize your food and service to
anyone who will listen, which I will do when I'm
unhappy, take heed. I'm not dreaming up dis-
pleasure. Its source lies in something you have

failed to do to make my eating experience as
enjoyable as I anticipated. You must find the
source and eliminate it or you will lose me and
my friends.

I insist on the right to dine leisurely, or eat
in haste, according to my mood, schedule or circumstances. I refuse to be rushed and I abhor
waiting. This is an important privilege that my
money buys from you. And if I'm not spending
big money with you this time, just remember that
if you treat me right, I'll be back with a larger
appetite and more money to spend. I may even
bring a few friends.

I'm much more sophisticated these days
than I was just a few years ago. I've grown accus-
tomed to better things and my needs are more
complex. I'm willing to spend more money with
you and I have more money to spend. But I
insist on quality to match your prices.

I am, above all, a human being. I'm sensi-
tive, especially when I'm spending money. I
can't stand being snubbed, ignored, or looked
down on. I'm proud. My ego needs the nourish-
ment of a friendly personal greeting from you.
It's important that you recognize my importance
to you and appreciate my business.

Of course, I'm a bit of a showoff. But don't
condemn me for that because you are probably a
little hammy at times yourself. Just smile and
indulge my whims as best you can. Remember
that while you are feeding me in the literal sense,

my money is figuratively feeding you.

Whatever my personal habits may be, you can be sure that I'm a nut on cleanliness in restaurants. Where food is concerned, I demand the strictest sanitation measures. I want my meals handled and served by the neatest people and on sparkling clean dishes. If I detect such carelessness as dirty fingernails, cracked dishes or soiled tables, you won't see me again.

I'm your customer now. But you must prove to me again and again that I have made a wise choice in selecting your restaurant over others. And you must repeatedly convince me that being a restaurant customer is a desirable thing in the first place. I can, after all, eat at home. But you must provide something more than food and service, something superior enough to beckon me away from my own table and draw me to yours. You must provide me the incentive to eat out.

THE RULES FOR PLAYING THE GAME OF LIFE

1. *You will receive a body.* You may like it or hate it, but it will be yours for your entire life.

2. *You will learn lessons.* You are enrolled in a full-time, informal school called life. Each day in this school you will have the opportunity to learn lessons. You may like the lessons or think them irrelevant and stupid.

3. *There are no mistakes, only lessons.* Growth is a process of trial and error and experimentation. The "failed" experiments are as much a part of the process as the experiment that ultimately "works."

4. *A lesson is repeated until it is learned.* A lesson will be presented to you in various forms until you have learned it. Then you can go on to the next lesson.

5. *Learning lessons does not end.* There is no part of life that does not contain lessons. If you are alive, there are lessons to be learned.

6. *"There" is no better than "here."* When your there has become a here, you will find another there that looks better.

7. Others are merely mirrors of yourself. You cannot love or hate something about another person unless it reflects to you something you love or hate about yourself.

8. What you make of your life is up to you. You have all the tools and resources you need. What you do with them is up to you.

9. The answers are there. The answers to life's questions are there to be found and understood. Ask God for the grace you need to find them—and then to recognize what you've found.

TRUE POWER
(Author unknown)

You may know me.
I'm your constant companion.
I'm your greatest helper.
I'm your heaviest burden.
I'll push you onward or drag you down to failure.
I'm at your command.
Half the tasks you do might as well
be turned over to me.
I'm able to do them quickly.
I'm able to do them the same every time.
I'm easily managed, all you've got to do
is be firm with me.
Show me exactly how you want it done;
And after a few lessons
I'll do it automatically.
I'm the servant of all great men and women;
Of course, I'm a servant of the failures as well.
I've made all the great individuals
who have ever been great.
And I've made all the failures, too.
I work with the precision of a computer
And with the intelligence of a human being.
You may run me for profit.
You may run me to ruin.
It makes no difference to me.
Be easy with me
And I'll destroy you.
Be firm with me
And I'll put the world at your feet.
Who am I?
I'm Habit!

BOSSES AND LEADERS
(Author unknown)

A boss drives.
A leader coaches.
A boss depends on authority.
A leader on goodwill.
A boss inspires fear.
A leader inspires enthusiasm.
A boss says, "I."
A leader says, "We."
A boss fixes blame.
A leader fixes problems.
A boss knows.
A leader shows.
A boss says, "Go."
A leader says, "Let's go!"

THE MAN WHO SOLD HOT DOGS

There was a man who lived by the side of the road and sold hot dogs. He was hard of hearing so he didn't have a radio. He had poor eyesight and so he never read the newspaper.

But he sold good hot dogs. He put up signs on the highway telling how good they were. He stood on the side of the road and cried, "Buy a hot dog, Mister?"

And people bought.

So he increased his meat and bun orders. He bought a bigger stove to take care of his trade. He finally got his son home from college to help him out. But then something happened. His son said, "Father, haven't you been listening to the radio, or reading the newspaper? There's a big recession. The Middle East is unsettled. The domestic situation is shaky."

Upon hearing this the father thought, "Well, my son's been to college, he reads the papers and listens to the radio, he ought to know."

So the father cut down his meat and bun orders, took down his advertising signs, and no longer bothered to stand out on the highway to sell his hot dogs.

And sure enough, his hot dog sales fell almost overnight. "You're right, son," the father said to the boy.

"We certainly are in the middle of a recession."

THE VALUE OF INTEGRITY

Long before Arthur Wellesley became the Duke of Wellington and defeated Napoleon at Waterloo, he had a character revealing encounter. After achieving a military victory in India in 1803, Wellesley met with the emissary of an Indian ruler who was anxious to know what territories would be ceded to his master as a result of the victory. Having tried various approaches without success, the emissary finally offered the general a bribe for the information.

Wellesley asked, "Can you keep a secret?"

"Yes, indeed," said the Indian eagerly.

"So can I," said Wellesley.

OPTIMISM

As a real estate agent was showing a couple a house he said, "This house has its good points and its bad points. To show you I'm honest, I'm going to tell you about both. The disadvantages are that there is a chemical plant one block north and a slaughterhouse one block south."

"What are the advantages?" inquired the prospective buyer.

"The advantage is that you can always tell which way the wind is blowing," replied the salesman.

KEEP YOUR FOCUS

Golf immortal, Arnold Palmer, once learned a painful lesson about overconfidence. It was the final hole of the 1961 Masters tournament, and had a one-stroke lead and had just hit a very satisfying tee shot. He felt he was in pretty good shape. As he approached his ball, he saw an old friend standing at the edge of the gallery. He motioned Palmer over, stuck out his hand and said, "Congratulations." Palmer took his hand and as he did, he knew he had lost his focus.

On his next two shots, he hit the ball into a sand trap, then put it over the edge of the green. He missed a putt and lost the Masters. "You don't forget a mistake like that," he said. "You learn from it and become determined that you will never do it again."

"NOT A ONE"

When young Timmy was in the third grade he was always a little slower than the other children. He fell behind in class and couldn't keep up on the playground.

As Valentine's Day approached, he told his mother, "I want to make a valentine for everyone in my class."

His mother hesitated because she knew Timmy wouldn't get a valentine from all of his classmates. She feared he might not get any.

But he persisted. And so his mother bought some paper, glue and crayons. Every night for a week Timmy labored. Each valentine was custom made and addressed.

When the big day arrived young Timmy left for school with a sack full of valentines. Fearing the worst, his mother made a batch of his favorite cookies. She had them sitting on the table with some cold milk, hoping to comfort her son when he got home.

When Timmy stepped off the bus his mother watched him walk toward their front door. As entered the house, Timmy shook his head from side to side and said, "Not a one. Not a one."

His mother's heart sank. Her son hadn't gotten a single valentine.

Timmy continued to repeat himself over and over. "Not a one. Not a one. I didn't forget a one."

Timmy will make a great grown-up someday, won't he?

A FINAL THOUGHT

"Give 'em the pickle" is really another way of saying, "Give 'em 100%" I learned this 100% principle from a Swedish Baptist Minister, Dave Danielson, whose course I was attending on marriage. He made the statement, "It's wrong to say a marriage is a 50/50 proposition. Men and women must give 100% of themselves to each other. That's what makes a marriage work.

After being married over forty years, it's the truth. No, I don't think anyone can give 100% of themselves all the time. But we should try.

Of course, there are nights when a husband or wife feel like clobbering each other. No two people ever get along all of the time. Yet, when you give 100%, and try to be unselfish, eventually you'll get around to smoothing out the waters.

The same is true of business. If we seek out a customer and give 100% we can be winners. And giving unselfishly like that means we give 'em the pickle whenever we can.

Thanks for reading this book. I hope you found it helpful and grow from it. And best of luck to you in your business, job, family and life.

Farrell's Pickle Production Inc.

Mr. Robert E. Farrell is one of the most impassioned customer service speakers in the country. His message has brought standing ovations to audiences in every part of the nation. If you're planing a corporate or association meeting and would like to consider him as a speaker, we'll gladly send you a sample video or audio cassette.

If you're company would benefit from a seminar, Mr.Farrell and his associate Bill Perkins, offer a half-day seminar entitled, "Building a Pickle Factory." This seminar helps companies develop a customer-service culture that treats customers so well they utter those three magic words, "I'll be back!"

For a copy of a video or audio cassette, or for more information, please write or call:
Farrell's Pickle Productions, Inc.
4120 N.E. Beaumont Street
Portland, OR 97212
1 (800) 200-7141

More Pickle Stories

I'm in the process of putting together a second book filled with pickle stories. If you, or someone in your company, has a fitting customer service story, please send it to me at the above address. I'll be sure and include your name and that of your company when the book is published.

A Special Mission

For over twenty years I've been involved with Young Life, a special mission that helps high school students. Every time a book is purchased a portion of the profits goes to support this ministry. I also contribute part of my speaking fees to Young Life.

I do this because I've seen this ministry turn around the lives of high school kids throughout the world. With their emphasis on friendship, fun, and spiritual truth this is a dynamic ministry. If you'd like more information about Young Life or what Young Life is doing in your area, please write me and I'll give you material that will answer your questions.

COMPANIES THAT GIVE AWAY PICKLES:

Alaska Airlines, Del Webb (Builder of Retirement Cities), Nike, Nordstrom, Oregon Trucking Association, Safeway, Inc., Sysco, The Dial Corp, U.S. Bank, Best Products Co., Farmers Insurance, Standard Insurance, Arthur Anderson, St. Vincent Hospital, NACM Oregon, Inc., Idaho Health Care Assoc., I.H.O.P. Corp., Marriott Corp., WESTA Assoc., Inc., William Pitt Jewelry Co., Portland Teachers Association, Department of the Army, National Restaurants Association, AT&T Customer Service Team, Bank of America, Pacific Corp, Pepsi Co., Commission for the Blind (USA), Cornell University, Gerber Advertising, Association of Oregon Industries, Gental Dentle, Grocers Insurance Group, GBD Architects, NorPac Foods Company, State Farm Insurance, Dale Carnegie Systems Co. Int., Oregon Dairy Association, Restaurants Unlimited, Wendy's International, United States Postal Service, Western Temporary Services, Saks 5th Avenue, Lomas Nettleson Co., HUD Agency (law), Safeco Insurance, United Grocers, Price Costco, Inc., Domino's Pizza, Mobil Oil, Reebok, Auto Owners Insurance, HWI Hardware, State Farm Insurance, Penn State University, Washington State Police, Oregon State Police, Lands End, Hooter's Restaurants, Caterpillar, Taco Time, Dain Bosworth, Bonneville Power Administration, and Coldwell Banker.